What No One Ever Tells You About

FRANCHISING

Real-Life Franchising Advice from
101 Successful Franchisors and Franchisees

Jan Norman

KAPLAN) PUBLISHING

President, Kaplan Publishing: Roy Lipner
Vice President and Publisher: Maureen McMahon
Senior Acquisitions Editor: Michael Cunningham
Development Editor: Karen Murphy
Production Editor: Leah Strauss
Interior Design: Lucy Jenkins
Cover Design: Rattray Design
Typesetter: Caitlin Ostrow

Library of Congress Cataloging-in-Publication Data

Norman, Jan.
    What no one ever tells you about franchising / Jan Norman.
      p. cm.
    Includes index.
    ISBN 1-4195-0613-7 (pbk.)
    1. Franchises (Retail trade) I. Title.
    HF4429.23.N676 2006
    658.8′708—dc22

                                               2005025365

DEDICATION

To God who does amazing things through ordinary people.

CONTENTS

SELECTING FRANCHISEES

FRANCHISE RELATIONSHIPS

FINANCING

GROWTH

PART 2. FRANCHISEES 83

PURCHASING ISSUES

FINANCING

MANAGEMENT

MARKETING

GROWTH

OVERCOMING TROUBLE

PART 3. EXPERTS   161

PREFACE

Franchising has become one of the most recognizable business formats in the world. Fundamentally, a franchisor supplies a system for operating a business, marketing and distributing products or services, and a brand; a franchisee provides money and elbow grease. It's an interdependent relationship that, at its best, makes both sides rich and at its worst destroys businesses and reputations.

Franchising is a method of doing business and distributing products or services that is used in more than 75 industries. In the United States alone more than 2,300 companies sell franchises and more than 767,000 individual businesses are franchises that have 9.7 million employees and $625 billion in annual revenues. Some sources cite even greater numbers, giving credit to franchising for jobs and an economic impact on the businesses that service franchises.

Despite those impressive data, franchising is carried out on the micro level. Don't let the dazzling statistics blind you to the fact that individual franchisors and franchisees fail. Their relationships can be acrimonious and even wind up in lawsuits, although probably no more so than in any other business endeavor created by human beings. Past abuses have led to federal and state laws making franchising more regulated than most individual industries.

The franchisors and franchisees who seem to be the happiest and most successful are dedicated to fairness and to the success of the other party as much as their own. Many of the people in franchising are passionate supporters. Many spend their careers moving among the different roles (some multiple times), at one time being a franchisor, at another a franchisee, and at yet another time becoming a consultant or supplier.

This book aims to give readers a sense of what franchising looks like in real life by illustrating common situations in real franchise companies. This is not theory; this represents some of the most typical ways that franchising plays out in real businesses. The purpose is not to glamorize or tear down franchising, but to show how to make franchising work to the benefit of the business owners and their customers. These franchisors and franchisees were selected for how they shed light on the process, not as endorsements for their specific brands. The franchisors range from the new, small, and unknown to some of the largest, best-known names in the world. Similarly, franchisees include one-location owners creating a lifestyle business to multiunit operators larger than many franchisors. I hope that owners of businesses who may be wondering if they should use franchising to expand will gain valuable information to help them decide if the role of franchisor is appropriate for them. I hope that individuals considering whether to buy a franchise will also envision how the struggles and triumphs of real franchisees may apply. I also hope each will read the other section and glean helpful insight about the other side of the franchising equation.

ACKNOWLEDGMENTS

Like all my books in the "What No One Ever Tells You" series, this book is the product of the generous help of hundreds of business owners. They are willing to share information because they want you, the reader, and in this case, the potential franchisor or franchisee, to succeed.

I have had wonderful help in finding the people and stories in this book. I am indebted to the International Franchise Association, American Association of Franchisees and Dealers, Profnet, National Association for the Self Employed, Terry Hill, Carol Markins, Beth Adkisson, Rhonda Sanderson, Christopher Bennett, Marcy Manning, Sarah Ryser, Meg Forehand, Nancy Russell, Michael Johnson, Jeff Louderback, Margaret Smallwood, Barbara Wiener-Fischhof, Dana Harville, Erin Del Llano, Alison Kenney, Les Winograd, Kahdijah Bell, Jenny Cherrytree, and Len Fischer.

PART 1

FRANCHISORS

. . .

Owners who want to expand their businesses often consider whether selling franchises will achieve their desired goals. Typically, those who give franchising a try instead of choosing internal growth through company-owned locations lack capital, skilled personnel, or time to achieve market penetration before being overrun by competitors. Franchising shares the risk of expansion with franchisees but also shares some control.

Not every business can be franchised successfully, though. First, the business must provide value for customers and franchisees. This means the original business is profitable and likely to survive a long time. It must also be a concept that appeals to people who buy franchises. This means prospective investors understand how the business makes its money and think they can do the same. The business must be capable of operating by a system that can be set out step by step, taught to others of average intelligence and skill, and succeed in various communities under a variety of economic circumstances. A franchisor must offer a business that is better than starting one from scratch and provide ongoing value so that the franchisee is still willing to pay royalties after learning how to run the business.

If you love running your own business, don't franchise. You will cease to be in that business, even if you continue to own some units. The franchisor's real business is making others successful at running the concept. The most successful franchisors continually find ways to add value for the franchisees. The franchisor has the greater power in the relationship and therefore the greater responsibility not to unfairly exploit that relationship. Far more laws have been passed to curb abuse by franchisors than by franchisees.

GETTING STARTED

■ ■ ■

Setting up a franchising company is complex and expensive. Before taking such action, honestly research whether your concept can be replicated. Consider whether you have the systems, competitive advantage, and brand to franchise. Analyze the competition. You can improve your opportunity for success with strategic partners and the right professional help. The cost of the franchise foundation tempts business owners to do it themselves, but the abundance of laws and regulations that govern franchising make it worth the money to do it right.

1. A CONCEPT THAT CAN BE FRANCHISED

Not every business has what it takes to create a franchise
system that can succeed in the increasing competition for
franchise buyers.

■ ■ ■

In the mid-1980s, Americans were crazy about frozen yogurt, an alternative to ice cream available only at specialty shops. The founders of one such shop, Penguin's Place Frozen Yogurt in Thousand Oaks, California, asked William Hawfield how to expand their business. He did a mountain of research, creating a three-inch-thick book of information about frozen yogurt, retailing, and franchising before agreeing to set up Penguin's franchise company.

As franchising has grown and succeeded for thousands of companies, thousands more have explored this avenue for growth. Many conclude the time, effort, money, and shift in emphasis from running a business to helping others run businesses is not right for their companies. Many others, including Penguin's, decide that it is.

For franchising to be a good growth vehicle, a business should have certain characteristics.

- It needs to prove its concept with a successful, profitable prototype store or office.
- It must have systems for doing every aspect of the business.
- It must be capable of being replicated in other markets.
- It should have a distinctive niche and brand to differentiate it from competitors.

Other companies had already proven the concept of franchising frozen yogurt shops, Bill says. "Penguin's had a successful prototype, but if it didn't grow, it would be overrun by the competition. At its heart, franchising builds distribution dominance. Most franchisors want to dominate a market quickly before others do it. Yet Penguin's founders didn't have enough money to grow on their own."

To use franchising as the growth vehicle, Penguin's needed the right products, a distinctive look, a financial model, ownership structure, and legal documentation, Bill says.

He looked at competing frozen yogurt shops and franchisors to assess how Penguin's could differentiate itself with quality frozen yogurt and a selection of toppings, a crisp black-and-white ambiance, and a competitive financial deal.

There certainly were some red flags, Bill says. Not only were other frozen yogurt retailers already franchising, but the cost of entry was relatively low, which would invite other competitors quickly. Existing dessert giants, such as Baskin-Robbins, already had nationwide distribution and could add frozen yogurt to compete directly with the newly popular specialty shops.

"Also, products have lifecycles, and we didn't know where frozen yogurt was in the cycle," Bill says. "My research and data suggested we were at the beginning, which was a green light."

Frozen yogurt grew quickly from $500 million in annual sales to $2 billion. That appeal indicated to Bill that competitors would join the market soon. Penguin's needed to establish its brand quickly and firmly. "From the beginning I told our people that we have to make this concept so strong that people will drive past six or seven other yogurt stores to come to Penguin's," he says. "Otherwise, convenience would rule, and we would not achieve the needed distribution."

Penguin's grew to 130 shops in three years, but in hindsight, Bill would have grown the franchising system even more quickly. "I found out that the value we as the franchisor created was brand distribution and dominance in a market; that's what the franchise buyers valued," he says. "I turned down opportunities to grow faster through (regional) development agreements, which would give up some (franchisor) control."

Penguin's eventually sold to a French dairy eager for a U.S. market through which to distribute its products. As grocery stores and other types of competitors entered the arena, many specialty frozen yogurt shops struggled and closed.

When making the decision whether to become a franchisor, Bill, now president of Hillcrest Associates, a Westlake Village, California, consulting firm, recommends weighing issues both of the heart and the head. "You need to be able to say, 'I love this and I'm going to commit everything to it.' But you also need hard data. Can this concept make money?" he says. "Don't do it without both."

2. CAREFUL DOCUMENTATION

A franchisor must be able to give franchisees detailed
instructions for best practices in running the business according
to a system that has proven successful in the past.

■ ■ ■

Heidi and Bion Flammang loved their dogs and wanted to build a business for dog owners who willingly spend a great deal of money to care for their pets. They were drawing up a business plan for a doggie day care center when Bion was killed in a plane crash in 1994. Heidi, a pharmaceutical sales representative, put the idea on the back burner and became a certified financial planner. But the concept nagged her, and in 2000 she opened the first Camp Bow Wow in Denver, Colorado.

At first, customers could drop their dogs off for the day, but the business was so successful that within six months Heidi expanded to offer overnight boarding. The dogs were kept in cabins, not pens. The employees were called counselors and were trained in dog psychology. The "campers" took afternoon naps in fleece-lined cots and if they misbehaved, they were given a time out. The camp included play equipment and a pool. Web cameras were placed around the camp so dog owners could check up on their pets while away. Heidi continued to add more services, such as caring for sick dogs and puppies, and providing vaccinations and grooming on site.

Every step of the way, Heidi kept careful records of every detail of building, stocking, and operating Camp Bow Wow. She opened a second camp after a year and envisioned operating four or five corporate-owned locations, so she needed the documentation and instructions for her store managers. Then a regular customer suggested she franchise the concept, and in 2003 she sold the first franchise.

The detailed documentation was essential, she says. "My files and documents were being used all the time, so when it came time to franchise I just had to formalize them a little to make them more user friendly," Heidi says. "I had to think through every single thing as if I had never done it before and make it as simple as possible. There are so many details: the way you clean and disinfect the kennels, the right size gravel so the dogs don't eat it."

A franchise with the best system in the world with repeated proven successes has little value if the franchisor does not set up the means to document and share the best practices for duplicating that success. The process of writing those documents helps improve and formalize the system, which improves it even more.

Even with great documentation, the process for opening and operating a Camp Bow Wow is continually evolving and the operations manual is being improved, Heidi says. "As I hire people with experience in other industries or franchises, it's amazing how they can improve it and take it to the next level."

One woman who used to work in the spa industry bought a Camp Bow Wow franchise. She created a four-way gate system, similar to that used for corralling cattle, for directing and funneling dogs into different areas of the kennel. It was a great improvement in the efficiency of operating a camp, Heidi says, so the gates were added to other locations.

Just as Heidi adds new ideas to improve the operating system, she drops things that don't work. "We are the support for our franchisees to make their lives easier. Anything that doesn't do that is dropped."

3. THE BENEFIT OF STRATEGIC ALLIANCES

Teaming with a well-known company can bring credibility,
quality, and price advantages to a franchisor.

■ ■ ■

Mary Rogers' name has been associated with education through franchising for more than two decades. Believing that children could benefit from quality technology training, Mary cofounded COMPUTER-TOTS and built it into the nation's largest children's computer education company with more than 150 buyers. After selling that company, she served as executive director of the Educational Foundation of the International Franchise Association for two years. Then she turned her attention to children's art education, launching Abrakadoodle in Reston, Virginia, with artist Lori Schue in 2002.

"Art has always been a passion of mine. It was my concentration in college," Mary says. "With the huge emphasis in schools on reading and math, programs like art have been cut, so there is a need."

As Mary and Lori were developing the Abrakadoodle model, they thought about other companies with which they could partner. One of the first names that came to mind was Crayola, owned by Binney & Smith, Inc., in Pennsylvania.

"In our classes we use a lot of Crayola products, so it was a logical choice," Mary says. "I went on their Web site and noticed that one of their initiatives is partnerships, so I contacted top-level managers and they passed my information on to Crayola's education division. That got the ball rolling."

Strategic alliances with the right partners can bring multiple benefits to a franchising company. In the case of a young company like Abrakadoodle, an alliance with an established brand name like Crayola brings enormous credibility. Binney & Smith has been making wax crayons for more than 100 years, and the Crayola brand is known worldwide.

Obviously, ties to an internationally known brand were valuable to Abrakadoodle. Crayola gave Abrakadoodle an exclusive license to use the Crayola trademark when advertising classes and franchises for sale. The two companies have mutual marketing programs. But Mary was looking for more. She wanted direct benefit for her franchisees.

"We wanted our franchisees to have product at discounted prices, plus we wanted quality control across the United States," Mary says. "Crayola has top quality products. If we didn't have this partnership, we put ourselves at risk. There could be very different outcomes in a class in the Bay Area of California from one in Boston if they used different quality of materials. Also Crayola products are 100 percent safe, and children's safety is absolutely important to our business."

However, alliances must be beneficial to both companies. Crayola values Abrakadoodle too. Not only is the art franchise a buyer of Crayola products, Mary says, "Crayola has a wonderful education division that has very definite ideas about how children should be taught art. They believe children should learn through a process and create a unique item, called process art. We're very strong in art education."

In her first face-to-face meeting with Crayola representatives, Mary brought her management team to demonstrate Abrakadoodle's experience despite the franchisor's youth as a company. Mary's success with COMPUTERTOTS and Lori's authorship of 11 books on children's art helped. Even when both companies agreed that the alliance would be mutually beneficial, the negotiations and legal documentation took months. The process went smoothly, Mary says, but still took time.

Crayola is unlikely to be Abrakadoodle's only strategic alliance. Mary is looking at several others, such as an art framing company that might give surplus mat board to Abrakadoodle in exchange for access to proud parents seeking to frame their children's art creations.

4. STICK TO A UNIQUE CONCEPT

A franchise is stronger if it focuses on doing one primary
business well instead of being all things to all people.

■ ■ ■

Marc Shuman and Skip Barrett ran a company that made retail store
fixtures. Because of the competition, they started looking for other uses for
a proprietary product called TekPanel. Of many possibilities, Marc chose
the untapped home garage organization market. In 2000, Marc and Skip incorporated GarageTek Inc. in Syosset, New York. A year later they started
selling franchises. One of the primary items a franchisor is selling is its
brand, and in brand development, Marc believes less is more.

GarageTek was the first national garage organization system of its
type. Rather than sell to every homeowner, Marc carved the niche more
narrowly, choosing to be "the Porsche of garage organization," targeting
the top 10 percent of earners in each market. "We won't do half a garage,"
he adds. "If a guy wants a few cabinets we recommend a local contractor.
Customers expect a GarageTek garage to be spectacular.

"I think a brand builds in a niche," Marc explains. "You're never going
to have a premium brand that serves the middle-class market or a middle-
class brand that serves the affluent. Pick one or the other. We give up sales
because of this approach, but you have to have the wherewithal to walk
away from the wrong market."

Marc also believes the company intent on building a strong brand must
resist the temptation to treat its product as a generic solution for all problems. "People try to get all the business they possibly can and dilute what
they stand for," he says. Some companies that started as closet organizers
have expanding into selling the same products for garages and home offices under the same name. "To me, that's a huge mistake," Marc says. "If
you are going to be the best in closets, do closets. Create a separate brand
and company for garages and a separate brand for home offices."

Marc acknowledges that the niche he has established for GarageTek
will prevent it from selling thousands of franchises. He figures he'll be for-
tunate to sell a hundred. At that point, he will pursue international markets
or create other brands in the home improvement market targeting affluent

consumers. "Anyone strong in brand management knows that consumers will give you credit for just one identity," Marc explains. "Procter & Gamble is king at this. That's why there's no such thing as Tide dishwashing soap. The Tide brand is only for laundry soap."

The separate franchises will have great cross-marketing opportunities. When the company reaches that stage, Marc anticipates creating a franchise holding company to manage all the different companies.

Creating a niche franchise forces the franchisor to niche its franchise sales as well. "It is very tempting for beginning franchisors to think that it's all about quantity," Marc says. "They put franchises where they don't belong or give away franchises for very low cost to induce people to buy a franchise. They think they're going to make up their profits in volume.

"Anybody can have 60 franchisees in two years; it's not tough to sell that many," he adds. "But their (franchisees) don't have blood in the deal. To them it's no big deal to walk away when it gets tough. We have restricted our sales (GarageTek adds about six new franchises a year) and as a result we have a strong system. We're not in every market, but we dominate the markets we're in."

5. GET PROFESSIONAL HELP

Franchising is so structured and regulated that the new franchisor must pay experts to set up systems and intellectual property protections correctly.

■ ■ ■

In 1999, Julie Collingsworth Hagenmaier was a pharmaceutical sales representative with a problem. Her husband was away on business and she was running so late that by the time she got her two-year-old daughter home from day care, the only food she found in the house for dinner was peas and popcorn. "At that point I decided I needed help, but the big concierge services didn't take you as a client unless you were employed by certain corporations with which they had contracts, and others had no professionalism or had a laundry list of rules," Julie says.

So she started her own personal concierge service, My Girl Friday, Inc., in Cincinnati, Ohio. Her target clients were busy professionals like herself who needed some help but couldn't afford a full-time nanny or assistant. By finding outside vendors My Girl Friday could clean the house, mow the lawn, walk the dog, set up the family Christmas tree, take the car to the repair shop, or dozens of other tasks. Clients and business executives encouraged Julie to franchise the concept and introduced her to franchise attorneys and consultants to help her build the legal, financial, and systems structures of a successful franchisor. She started selling My Girl Friday franchises in 2004.

"Professional help is so key," Julie says. "Franchising is not a one-person show like running a small business. You need experts to help you through the process, and you will have to pay for them . . . It seems that daily I am talking to either an attorney, an accountant, or a banker about something related to franchising."

Every business ought to be set up professionally and legally, but systems and legalities are mandatory for a franchisor. Both the Federal Trade Commission and state agencies regulate franchising. Companies that try to license their business to others informally can get into tremendous legal trouble. Potential franchise buyers must receive a Uniform Franchise Offering Circular (UFOC) that must be a carefully crafted legal document. But that's just the beginning, Julie says. "Anything you say to buyers you have to prove, so I have to be very careful," she says. "I'm working on the company vision every day, but I can't make visionary statements."

Initially, My Girl Friday had a general business attorney, but trademarks, slogans, and other intellectual property weren't properly protected, Julie says. As My Girl Friday started entering other states, the franchisor had to sue other companies using the same or similar names before it could sell franchises. "Franchise law is so complex, with audits and UFOCs, that experts are less expensive and do better work than general lawyers," says Julie, who hired New York franchise attorney Harold Kestenbaum and iFranchise Group, an Illinois consulting specialist.

At one point, Julie was dealing with 11 different attorneys, from intellectual property experts to tax specialists. "Whatever you think you will spend on attorneys, triple it," she advises. She has also tapped the expertise of marketing and business management experts. "You think you're going to start a business doing what you love. You do that in the beginning, but you eventually have to run the business . . . you start doing all the things that you don't have a clue about," Julie says. "Then you have to hire people to perform the projects, hire people to manage them, and create relationships with bankers and hire lawyers and more lawyers."

---

6. ANALYZE THE COMPETITION BEFORE FRANCHISING

A franchise system must be capable of being replicated *and* have differentiation from the competition in order to be successful.

■ ■ ■

When David Hearld almost lost his business because of embezzlement, he decided to work with vendors to pay them back rather than file for bankruptcy. His suppliers were so impressed that they referred their other financially distressed customers to David for help with their workout. On these businesses' behalf, David was dealing with a lot of impatient collections attorneys. "I needed a message that would keep them on hold until I got to the phone," David says. "Based on what I know now, it was a horrible message. It told about my history and some clients. But I noticed even the first day a huge change in these attorneys. They stayed on the line and treated me with more respect." That experience eventually led David to create Profit-Tell International in Hinsdale, Illinois, as an audio marketing and advertising service in 1993.

The marketplace is full of companies providing background music, on-hold messages, and in-store promotional announcements. Profit-Tell needed more in order to be a viable business, let alone a system that could be franchised. While much of the competition offered standard messages sold over the Internet and no support staff, Profit-Tell offered custom messages and plenty of face-to-face customer service. It marketed itself as an audio marketing company, not just a recording studio for on-hold messages. David researched ways to improve the effectiveness of audio marketing and came up with a 25-point process for scripts that worked. Any script that didn't score at least 21 points was rewritten. Although David considered himself a great salesman, he couldn't even persuade his best friends to buy Profit-Tell services initially, so he developed a different selling system.

When the background music pioneer Musak tried to buy Profit-Tell, David realized he had something with potential. He analyzed growing the company through a corporate sales team, licensing, or franchising and concluded that trained franchisees who owned and operated their own businesses would provide the high level of customer service and specialized sales approach David wanted. "I'd rather take someone as a franchisee with good customer service skills than an experienced salesman. Salesmen think they're good, but they don't know how to sell this product and they're hard to change."

Profit-Tell helps franchisees become marketing consultants, not merely sellers of audio advertising. The franchisor has added audio products for Web sites, for overhead announcements in stores, and CDs to its initial telephone on-hold scripts. Although Profit-Tell doesn't produce brochures, advertising, and telephone directory ads, franchisees can submit these materials from their clients to the franchisor, which evaluates their marketing effectiveness. The franchisor also has a script department to write effective audio marketing scripts, based on David's 25-point process, voice-over talent and rights to music, so franchisees don't have to find their own. "Franchisees have to see value added; for the franchisor that's the key," David says. "Competitors can sell for less so we have to provide and sell added value. First we have to make it easy for our franchisees and their clients. We have to give clients more than they expect. If you don't have a niche or different approach, you won't succeed."

7. THE ACCIDENTAL FRANCHISOR

Some companies get into franchising as the result of circumstance.

■ ■ ■

Canadian entrepreneur Jack Lee lived for more than 20 years in Australia where he built one of the country's largest landscape and horticulture companies that designed and constructed golf courses and commercial landscaping. When his father became ill, Jack returned to Canada and brought with him the rights to be the master franchisee in Canada for Mini-Tankers International, an on-site diesel refueling concept that originated in Australia. In 1995, Jack opened Mini-Tankers Canada Ltd. in Langley, British Colombia.

"I was the first external licensee; it was more a concept than a system at that point," Jack says. "Once I set up there was even less to it than I thought, but I was committed to making it work." Many people buy a franchise because they don't know how to run a company. That wasn't Jack's concern because he had been in business for himself his entire adult life. He thought the concept of delivering fuel to customers had a great deal of opportunity. Still he was paying royalties for a franchise that had no system of doing business and no trademark value. The franchisor didn't even have a brochure. Jack made his own videos and other marketing materials, and built a large information technology system and database to run his company. In essence, he wound up building a system both for himself and the franchisor. "I could have rescinded (the franchise agreement) but that's not my style. I had a moral contract," he says. "If I sat on my hands, I wouldn't build value for myself either."

The franchisor went bankrupt in 2003, an occurrence over which Jack had no control and could have been a disaster for his own business. He had to decide whether to walk away from the hard work he had put into the system in order to build his own business or to invest even more money into becoming the franchisor himself. Jack bought back rights to his own company, the systems he developed, the name Mini-Tankers in Canada only, and franchising rights in that country. He could sell franchises as before, but agreed not to expand outside Canada until 2006. "There was no price break for the value I had brought into the business," he says. "My attitude is, if there is a problem, fix it. Blame is a negative emotion. Bite the bullet and move on." However, Jack does advise other franchise buyers to investigate and make sure the franchisor—especially a new one—has a proven system to avoid the situation he encountered.

Mini-Tankers Canada refuels trucks, buses, trains, ships, boats, and heavy equipment at customers' locations. Companies with fleets of vehicles used to have drivers stop on their routes to refuel. Mini-Tankers franchisees deliver diesel fuel, oil, and lubricants, often at night, so that customers don't have to spend work time refueling the vehicles and equipment and don't have to maintain storage tanks on their property. The franchisor manages and monitors customers' fuel consumption by computer so they never run out of diesel, which would cause costly down time.

In 2005, he changed the name of the company to 4Refuel so that he would have the same brand worldwide when he expanded outside Canada. "The opportunity is huge, but I'm glad I didn't know all the problems because the concept is really good," he says. "If I had known everything, I might not have done it."

MANAGEMENT
■ ■ ■

The franchising company cannot be run like the concept it is created to grow. The franchisor is now in the business of selling franchises and supporting franchisees. It must maintain the integrity and value of the brand, control quality at all levels, and continually find ways to improve and build upon the system that attracts and keeps franchisees. As in other types of business, things can go awry for franchisors. You must make adjustments. Franchising offers shared responsibility and opportunity, making it suitable for entities beyond restaurants. However, franchising still is not right for every company.

8.   BUILD THE BRAND

All elements of a business should contribute to making a
distinctive brand that enhances the value of the franchise.

■ ■ ■

When Tim Timoteo opened R.J. Gator's Florida's Sea Grill and Bar, a beer and wine restaurant in Jupiter, Florida, in 1986, he wasn't intentionally laying the groundwork for a successful regional franchising company.

But his previous two decades' experience in the restaurant industry taught him that R.J. Gator's needed to be more than a name. It needed to be a strong, distinctive brand that touched everything from the atmosphere to the menu to the work culture.

"Every entrepreneur with a product or service can have a successful brand if (he) can differentiate it from the masses," Tim says. "There are many casual dining restaurants. What we had to do was find something that no one else was doing."

The result, R.J. Gator's Florida's Sea Grill and Bar. The ambiance is Florida Everglades. The restaurant looks like a woodsy lodge with a porch. Stuffed alligators and murals of Everglade scenes decorate the walls. The staff wears safari shorts and bright-colored shirts. The logo is a caricature of an alligator in a hat and sunglasses carrying a food tray.

Others offer Tex-Mex food or a broad American menu. R.J. Gator's features Florida specialty foods and gives them a unique twist. It is about the only place selling alligator tail, which is tenderized and marinated for a distinctive flavor. R.J. Gator's menu also includes Havana banana chicken with black beans and rice, handmade coconut shrimp, and sweet plantains.

Even the language is part of the brand. Appetizers are called "gatorizers." One of the drinks is a 32-ounce "gatorita." One of the desserts is gator tail pie. The waiters are Everglades' guides.

"I relate our business to Disney," Tim says. "We're not really in the restaurant business. We sell an experience. People are so busy that when they go out to eat they want an experience that is memorable. That's what a brand is. If your restaurant is like everyone else's, it's a commodity that's not worth a franchise buyer's money. Our brand gives our franchisees a competitive edge."

R.J. Gator's original restaurant was so well received that customers started asking to buy franchises. Tim complied in 1991, sticking with the brand he originally developed. The chain remains in the Southeast. "I'm not going too far away from our home base of brand awareness," Tim explains. "We want to saturate Florida and have a critical mass in each market we enter."

A franchisor's brand should extend beyond decorations and clever names on the menu to the entire culture of the business, Tim says. Each R.J. Gator's restaurant strives to become part of the local community, supporting local charities, closing on Thanksgiving to feed the homeless, collecting toys for children at Christmas. R.J. Gator's has given thousands of dollars to cancer research since Tim's wife and partner Joan died of lung cancer several years ago.

"The brand is about people connecting with people," Tim says. "We let people know that we're here to make the community better. I find the more I give, the more I get back. I wouldn't sell a franchise to people who weren't willing to close their restaurant on Thanksgiving to feed the homeless. I have found that a lot of franchise buyers want to get involved in such things but don't know how. We guide them."

9. TWEAK THE SYSTEM

Slow growth when the company is young allows modifications
to ensure a stronger, long-lasting system over time.

■ ■ ■

Larry Green and Doug Lueck each had experience building patios and driveways with interlocking stones before they teamed up to start Systems Paving Inc. in Newport Beach, California, in 1992. Even with double-digit sales growth every year, the partners expanded slowly, making sure to establish the right operational systems, employee training, and measurement tools before taking the next step.

Larry, who had a company that installed interlocking stones in South Africa for 14 years, knew how to run a business and build patios and driveways. He wanted to make sure his knowledge transferred to another country. Doug worked for a similar company in the United States. He wanted to strengthen his business ownership skills.

Even when the pair decided to open more offices, they didn't use franchising at first. They created Systems Paving University initially for sales personnel and later added training for field supervisors and construction managers. They established methods to convert satisfied customers into referrals for more business. They developed a direct-mail advertising campaign that could be duplicated in any market. They created proprietary software to track the progress of individual jobs and another software program that gave homeowners a three-dimensional simulation of their residence with paving-stone driveways and patios. Each system and tool was designed to make the company operate efficiently and manage growth of satellite offices.

"We gave managers of those offices a lot of autonomy and when we looked at the structure and operation, they looked a lot like franchises," Larry says.

Finally, in 2001, Systems Paving tested its first franchise in carefully selected locations including Massachusetts.

The slow, steady development of systems enabled Systems Paving to refine the systems and franchising model before becoming more active in selling franchises nationwide. "We started slow because we wanted to learn this business," Doug says. "And we proceeded slowly with franchising to figure that out too."

The partners' experience with their own stores convinced them that franchisees didn't necessarily have to be construction experts. They needed sales and management skills. So those were the experiences they looked for in franchise buyers, and those topics dominate the initial and ongoing franchise training.

The company-owned stores built revenues to $30 million by 2004, so that Systems Paving didn't need to sell franchises to survive. "You should make sure you have something real in place so you don't have to sell franchises to survive," Larry says.

Even after Systems Paving started selling franchises, "we made some tweaks to the franchise model so that we could grow more quickly," Larry says. One modification is the size of a franchise territory, currently 50,000 single-family residences. Each area needs to encompass enough upscale homes to assure the franchisee of strong sales, but not so large that the brand doesn't penetrate quickly and strongly.

Systems Paving can do well by selling three to five franchises a year. Larry estimates that eventually 200 franchises will be enough to cover the United States adequately.

Being systematic and slow to build Systems Paving will make the franchisor stronger over the long term, Larry insists. "Franchising has made us even better. It brings people with a pride of ownership. That's better than just being an employee. Our franchisees don't work until the shift is over; they work 'til the job is done. When you bring in good people, it helps our own operations too."

10.   LEARN FROM OTHERS' MISTAKES

When building your franchise system, study the weaknesses in other franchisors as well as their successes.

■ ■ ■

Richard Rennick started working for his father's plumbing business while still a teenager. After researching methods for detecting water, sewer, oil, and air leaks without tearing a building apart, he started American Leak Detection in Hemet, California, in 1974, and later moved it to Palm Springs, California. During the first four years, he continued his day job as a policeman and put his salary into research and development. In 1979, he started selling dealerships, and in 1984, he started selling franchises, convincing dealers to convert to franchisees.

"One of the things I did when studying franchise organizations was instead of looking at successes like McDonald's, which was *the* success story back then, I looked at ones that were not successes," Dick says. "Franchising had been around a hundred years, yet it was still in the fledgling stage at that time."

During the 1970s and 1980s, in many cases, the relationship between franchisor and franchisee was more adversarial. Dick noticed some common factors among franchisors that struggled or had contentious relations with franchisees. Some franchisors would write their contracts in ways that financially disadvantaged their franchisees, he says. Other franchisors would take money from the marketing fund to meet payroll, which meant less brand-building advertising and resulted in franchisee lawsuits. Dick was determined not to follow in those footsteps.

"These (failed) franchisors wouldn't share with their business partners, the franchisees," Dick says. "I decided the relationship between franchisor and franchisee is paramount. I think American Leak Detection has one of the better names in franchising for having a balanced system, a win-win situation."

For example, American Leak Detection has spent a great deal of money developing proper equipment, which it makes only for its franchisees. It does not do any outside sales. When American Leak Detection saturated the United States market, it started selling franchises in foreign countries rather than encroach into the operating territories of existing franchisees to sell more domestic franchises.

Dick's approach has been recognized on both sides of the fence. Dick has been honored by the International Franchise Association as entrepreneur of the year and was IFA chairman in 2005. American Leak Detection adheres to the IFA's code of conduct. At the same time, the company has earned the Fair Franchising Seal from the American Association of Franchisees and Dealers. To earn the seal, at least 74 percent of franchisees in a system must approve, but for American Leak Detection 98 percent of its franchisees voted in favor of the franchisor receiving the seal. American Leak Detection was rated number one in franchisee/franchisor relations by *Success* magazine in 2000.

"If we have disputes, we hit them head on," Dick says. "Our advisory council (of franchisees) helps with some issues. We ferret out solutions that work for everyone. Some things I won't let go of. For one, I must be the protector of the brand. Another is compliance with customer service. If the need arises, we will go in and resolve a problem when a customer and franchisee can't come to terms. If necessary, we will bring in a mediator. That happened just once in more than 20 years."

As a result of learning what not to do from franchising failures, Dick built an international success. "I allow the system to be entrepreneurial," he says. "I don't try to control the entrepreneurs; I try to guide them."

11. TECHNOLOGY IS A TOOL

Technology, properly used, can improve every aspect of franchise operation.

■ ■ ■

Debbie Gordon was a technology consultant selling women's shoes on eBay as a hobby in 2002 when the entrepreneur in her thought this could be a business. Unlike the people who move from hobbyist to super seller on eBay in an effort to grow their businesses, Debbie started Snappy Auctions in Nashville, Tennessee, in 2003 to handle eBay sales for others who are too busy or uninterested to do it themselves. Part of the concept is to have a store where customers can drop off their merchandise. Each must be priced at $50 or higher. If an item sells, Snappy Auctions handles shipping and payment, taking 15 percent to 35 percent of the selling price. If it doesn't sell, the customer can pick it up or it is donated to charity.

The technology is the measurable point of differentiation, both for the customer and for the franchisee. Technology also enables Snappy Auctions to streamline all its franchising functions.

"My background in technology was on the strategy level: how to use technology to improve business," Debbie says. "I knew what technology could do."

She brought in top-notch software programmers to develop software that is the core of Snappy Auctions' operations and franchising. The software streamlines the entire process from accepting new inventory to direct listing on eBay, from printing FedEx shipping labels addressed to the winning bidder to accepting PayPal payments.

"We had to build a system to integrate the information to all three of those corporations so we don't have to enter information three times," she says. "The software is a customer database, an inventory management system, a bookkeeping service for each store. We are able to monitor our customers, who they are, their age, gender, zip code, and income. Franchisees can (use the software to) manage their profit and loss information."

The software is a quantifiable benefit for franchisees, Debbie says. Some franchisees have asked whether they can sell their own items on eBay outside of Snappy Auctions, but the software is so efficient that they save money by selling through Snappy Auctions even after paying the commission.

"It's one thing to say 'we have a brand and image, blah, blah.' But the software is a difference they can measure in dollars," Debbie says.

Snappy Auctions saved money by creating its own software and related technology in-house, she says. The franchisor was also able to customize the technology to streamline other functions besides the eBay auction process. Snappy Auctions doesn't have to audit its franchisees' financial information because the software automatically tracks it. That saves not just money but also avoids potential arguments with franchisees over money issues, Debbie says.

Snappy Auctions applies technology to the franchise sales process, an increasingly popular technique for franchisors. "We have so streamlined selling franchises through technology that it filters out a lot of junk," she adds. "It used to be that someone called a franchisor, and then someone had to call them back, mail a brochure, and follow up. Most prospects find us online. They fill out our form online. We get the information immediately and e-mail back the information they want. Everything is done electronically so it doesn't require a lot of salespeople."

12. MARKETING PROGRAMS

No one marketing tool builds business, but a combination of
efforts boost sales and strengthens the brand.

■ ■ ■

Wireless Toyz in Farmington Hills, Michigan, is in a pitched battle with aggressive national companies for purchasers of cell phones, pagers, satellite television, and accessories. It cannot match its competition on television advertising, but its total marketing package can differentiate Wireless Toyz with the help of franchisees.

"Most of our marketing is direct mail," says Richard Simtob, partner and chief operating officer. "We target people with a price on the phones that is cheaper than the competition just to pull people into the stores. Then we make money on the accessories and the calling plan they buy."

Wireless Toyz was one of the first nonexclusive wireless retailers in the United States. Its stores offer five different cell phone carriers and two satellite providers. Its customer service, which is a key component of marketing, must be superior to the national wireless companies in order to win customers. "Customers want unbelievable service and don't want to go to 12 different locations (to comparison shop)," Richard says. Wireless Toyz offers such enticements as referral credits and volume purchase discounts. Perhaps more important, its franchisees and their sales staffs provide knowledge and a willingness to compare competing plans to find the best for the customer. "We can't just sell someone something. They have to be a customer for the service we sell them at least six months or we don't get our commission," Richard explains. "Service is everything."

Most franchisors hold annual conferences. Wireless Toyz holds two conferences a year and insists that franchisees attend. "If you can't leave for three days, you don't own the business, the business owns you," Richard says. "People get so pumped up that sales go up when they return to their stores." The most popular sessions at these conferences feature panels of top Wireless Toyz franchisees explaining how they operate to maximize sales.

"None of us in this company could put this together alone but take one idea from 20 guys and everyone benefits," Richard says. "Everyone comes up with fantastic marketing ideas."

Often customers have to wait for service in Wireless Toyz stores. One franchisee put in a cooler full of water, sodas, and snacks. "It's like saying, 'welcome to my home.' We implemented it quickly just by telling franchisees about it. Customers feel like they're getting something extra."

Another franchisee set up a play table to keep children of customers occupied while their parents shop. The result is higher sales because parents, especially mothers, don't feel rushed by their bored children. Now the play area is mandatory in every store. Some franchisees have augmented that idea with free balloons for customers' children.

One store started giving away free Wireless Toyz T-shirts with every purchase. Customers wore them shopping, to the gym, working in the yard, or to Little League games, which spread Wireless Toyz's name all over town. A third of the franchisees have adopted that idea.

The franchisor has a costume that looks like a cellular telephone that franchisees can buy. They hire a young worker to wear the costume and stand on the street to wave drivers toward the store. Some franchisees use it; others don't. The franchisor provides grand opening flyers and materials, a national toll-free number for routing customer calls to the nearest store, discount rates for the direct mailer program, on-hold telephone recordings, and co-op marketing programs that franchisees can choose to use or not.

"We're constantly coming up with more creative marketing ideas," Richard says. "There are so many things we do. No one thing explains it but together we calculate that they account for at least a 20-percent increase in sales."

13. THE NEVER-ENDING NEED TO BE FLEXIBLE

When your industry or markets change, remaining static is fatal.

■ ■ ■

Personal computers were exploding in popularity for individual consumers when Lonnie Helgerson started The Computer Doctor in Aberdeen, South Dakota, as a mobile computer repair service in 1992. Lonnie was familiar with technology retailing because he had worked at MicroAge and ComputerLand in the 1980s. He was familiar with franchising because he was working for Super 8 Motels when he launched The Computer Doctor. Without dropping mobile services, The Computer Doctor added retail stores to sell computers, ink cartridges, ribbons, and anything else consumers asked for. With a fixed location, Lonnie didn't have to go out and find business; it came walking through the door. He started selling franchises in 1996, and with the massive outlays for new computer technology leading up to 2000, The Computer Doctor had 70 franchisees with 150 stores.

"Technology is fast changing. It's like bananas. If it sits on the shelf an hour it goes bad," Lonnie says. He foresaw trouble ahead for The Computer Doctor as technology prices plunged and profit margins dwindled to zero. Ninety percent of the chain's customers were new each month. It was impossible to build long-term relationships with customers. Lonnie had to move to rebrand and reposition the company. He worked with his franchisee advisory council to restructure.

The real money and repeat business for technology was in business-to-business transactions, but the name "The Computer Doctor" sounded unsophisticated, so the first move Lonnie made in 2002 was to change the company brand to Expetec, a combination of expedited and technology. That was merely symbolic of the greater change from retail storefronts to more services and from individual to business customers.

One change was financial. Individual customers pay immediately; businesses pay in 30 to 60 days. Many of the franchisees didn't have cash reserves to be able to let go of the instant cash fix even though the business sales were much larger. "What I didn't understand was that the shift from the individual consumer coming into the store to Expetec franchisees going out into the businesses was so dramatic that most of the franchisees couldn't make the jump," Lonnie says. "Many of our franchisees weren't willing to change with us because they feared that cutting out retail traffic would kill their businesses."

He offered to let franchisees out of their agreement if they didn't want to work within the new model. Only ten remained. Looking back, Lonnie says he should have worked hard to sell the new model to all his franchisees, shown them how they would benefit and make much more money, and made sure they remained in the system. Instead, "it was like starting over," he says.

Within three years the company, now located in Lake Mary, Florida, was back to 70 franchisees. They tend to have multiple units and have more capital than Lonnie's initial group of The Computer Doctor franchisees. "More are business managers than techies," he says. "They're more apt to have worked for IBM Global Services than in their own shop. They are more familiar with working with business clients with thousands of computers. Our business is better suited for the future. Unfortunately, not everyone bought into the idea along the way. I lost many good relationships with franchisees as a result of my decision."

14. THE IMPORTANCE OF COMPANY-OWNED STORES

The franchisor should prove the concept with its own units before selling franchises and should use company-owned units for ongoing experimentation and validation.

■ ■ ■

Bob Schambaum owned several shoe stores and had trouble finding quality signs for his business. So he asked his friend Gary Salomon, who owned six different businesses, to look at a sign shop for possible purchase. "The shop had a lot of technology and I realized it had the potential to do for the sign industry what quick printing did for the print industry," Gary says. The pair bought FASTSIGNS in July 1985, opened a second store six months later and a third seven months after that.

"We tested the concept several times by opening three company stores with our own money," Gary says. "At the end of that period, we were leaning toward franchising but we were willing to look at doing more company stores."

Before franchising, a business owner should test the concept himself and know how it operates inside out, Gary says. It should be a concept and not just a fad with long-term potential. It should be a concept that the average person can learn and operate and gross six figures within five years. FASTSIGNS fit all those requirements. But the real motivation to franchise was the realization that the business was really a custom job shop with a lot of complexity. It required a high level of customer service, attention to detail, outside sales skills, and the ability to deal with technology and light manufacturing. Store managers, at the salary Gary and Bob could afford, just didn't have the commitment, drive, and maturity to grow the business.

"My partner and I would open a store and work there, but as soon as we left to go to the next store, things didn't go well," Gary says. "Ultimately, this is an owner-operated business."

Gary and Bob might not have realized why they needed ownership of individual stores and the type of owner that person should be if they had not thoroughly tested the concept in their own stores first. "I don't think you have a lot of credibility unless you have owned and operated stores first," Gary says. "When we toured (potential franchise buyers) through headquarters, we usually showed them the company-owned store. The level of access we had was more certain than at a franchise store. And we had a level of confidence about how the store would look at any given time so there were no surprises."

In some franchise systems, the franchisees object that the company-owned units compete with them or that the franchisor cherry picks the best locations. If the franchisor retains ownership, it must be careful about how many stores it owns and their location relative to franchisees.

FASTSIGNS kept ownership of one store as it sold hundreds of franchises internationally. When new franchisees came to headquarters for training, they were able to spend some time with hands-on experience in the company shop which boosted their confidence in being able to handle real business situations. For the first 15 years, Gary also used the company store to test new equipment, technology, and other ideas for improving the business before rolling them out to franchisees. In recent years, FASTSIGNS, headquartered in Carrollton, Texas, started having technologically savvy franchisees handle the tests.

"You have to be patient as franchisees adapt to whatever changes you want to make to the system" Gary says. "There is a whole spectrum of owners, and you can't make changes on a dime. That is very different from how an entrepreneur handles change. The biggest challenge for me was going from the entrepreneur to structured-business mindset. A franchisor must make a transition to realize that you can't undermine the infrastructure that you have in place."

15. TAKE CHARGE OF SITE SELECTION

The franchisor usually has more experience and leverage to
find and acquire the best sites for its franchisees.

Location can be the single most important factor of success in certain types of franchises, such as retail and restaurants. Farmer Boys, which started with the turn around of a poorly performing restaurant in Perris, California, in 1981, had repeated success in finding locations for its next seven company-built restaurants. But by 1997, the founders, brothers Makis and Chris Havadjias, realized that to continue the growth, their Riverside, California, company would need the vehicle of franchising.

"One assumption we made was that every franchisee would come to the table ready, willing, and able to find his own real estate," says Don Tucker, director of franchising for the sit-down and drive-through chain that serves hamburgers, sandwiches, and full breakfasts. "In reality, we have had to be much more participatory in finding locations."

Like other franchisors, Farmer Boys always had the final approval of a franchise location, so there was never the fear that a franchisee would try to put a restaurant in the middle of the desert, Don says. The franchisor provided some guidelines to finding successful locations, but those criteria have become more refined as the chain has grown. A good Farmer Boys site will be in middle-income neighborhoods where there is both a daytime working crowd at factories, offices, and stores and a residential area. The street has high traffic, and the site itself has easy access, adequate parking for customers who choose to eat at the restaurant, and enough real estate for the mandatory drive-through window. Also, of course, it's best if there's minimal competition nearby. In many communities, such sites are increasingly scarce.

"There's a misperception among franchisees who look around and think a corner would be a good place for a Farmer Boys," Don says. "But they don't realize that it doesn't have enough parking, or the city won't allow a drive through. Then the franchisee gets discouraged." Farmer Boys also learned in the early years that many commercial real estate brokers and landlords do not want to deal with individual franchisees. They only want to deal with the corporation and to have the franchisor on the lease in case a single franchisee doesn't succeed, Don says. So, Farmer Boys Food, Inc., corporate office has had to take the lead role in finding and negotiating sites for its franchisees.

"Some franchisors will sign up anyone anywhere and worry later about whether they can make it. They just want growth," Don says. "Our growth strategy was different. We consciously decided to start only in Southern California. If someone from Kansas City came to visit and wanted to buy a franchise, we would not sell it. We're not going to Kansas City until it's right for the system. We want economies of scale, the ability to cluster units in a geographic area, and brand name recognition."

Farmer Boys started approving area developers for cities outside Southern California, such as Las Vegas, Nevada, and Phoenix, Arizona. Some of those developers have real estate experience with other franchise concepts and don't need the franchisor's site location help, Don says, but others do.

The franchisees' reaction to Farmer Boys becoming more active in real estate decisions has been mixed. Some expect and appreciate the help of getting approvals from cities, water and sewer districts, and utilities. But some wonder why the process takes one to two years, even though the franchisor cautions about the delays early in the franchise purchasing process. "The individual who wants to be in business for himself is not interested in waiting two years before starting to generate income," Don says. "And they blame us. But any franchisee who goes through the process himself the first time really appreciates what we do when they buy a second unit."

16. OWNERSHIP OF PRODUCTS SOLD THROUGH FRANCHISES

A franchisor's restriction of products used or sold by
franchisees can aid consistency and add income but can also
be a source of disagreement.

■ ■ ■

Stan Krempges was a partner in a company that built wooden fences. His customers would spend thousands of dollars on fences for their homes and naturally wanted products to protect and preserve the wood. At the same time, Stan's own home had wooden decks and cedar siding that he wanted to protect. So he worked with a chemist to develop an environmentally safe cleaner to restore wood's original beauty, and a protectant to prevent future damage by rain, wind, and weather, as well as procedures for using them in the most effective, cost-efficient ways. Stan started a home-based business, Woodbrite, in Springfield, Missouri, in 1993, to sell and apply the products. He changed the name to Wood Re New in order to obtain a nationally protected trademark and started franchising in 2001.

One requirement in the franchise agreement is to use the specially formulated Wood Re New cleaner, protectant, and all-purpose cleaner. "We have two reasons," Stan says. "One, we want consistency among all Wood Re New locations, and two, it is a revenue stream (for the franchisor), not so much now but it will be as the system grows."

Many franchisors require franchisees to buy products or equipment through the franchisor as a means of assuring consistency and quality and of protecting guarantees of any results promised by company marketing to all customers. The franchisor wants to be sure that its product is the same at every location. If franchisees were allowed to substitute low-priced but inferior ingredients or other items essential to delivering the core products, the brand would be diminished and other franchisees harmed. This requirement works best when the mandatory products are within the franchisor's area of expertise. In addition, some franchisors require franchisees to buy nonessentials, such as stationary or napkins, through the central office. In some cases, franchisors negotiate bulk rates that are cheaper than an individual franchisee can find on its own, but in other cases, franchisor prices are higher. Some franchisors use product or equipment purchasing restrictions to boost their own bank accounts at the expense of franchisees. This practice is a source of animosity between franchisor and franchisees. Many experts recommend that franchisees be allowed to buy goods or services from other sources if they are of acceptable quality and don't harm the trademark or reputation of the franchisor. On the other hand, these experts acknowledge that franchisor-supplied products may be more efficient and effective, especially in systems like Wood Re New where the products are the basis of differentiation the franchise has from competitors. "They have been chemically developed to restore and maintain wood's natural appearance no matter the age of the wood," Stan says.

"It's typical for franchisees to want to try their own ideas, but you have to wonder why did they buy a franchise," Stan says. "They get bombarded by salesmen who claim they have a product that works better in different areas of the country. There have been a few franchisees that we have had to help see the value of our exclusive products."

17. BUSINESS FORMAT THAT WORKS BEYOND MAIN STREET

Nonprofit organizations can benefit from the systems, brand,
and consistency that franchising offers.

■ ■ ■

Wayne and Diane Tesch started a one-week summer camp to give a positive experience to abused children, most of them in foster care, in Orange County, California, in 1985. Newport Mesa Christian Center in Costa Mesa sponsored the 37 children and provided the 12 counselors and nine additional staff. Within five years churches in Lakewood, California, and Phoenix, Arizona, opened Royal Family Kids' Camps, following the Tesches' successful prototype.

"The need was overwhelming," Wayne says. "Orange County had 10,500 reported cases of child abuse in 1985 and we took 37 to camp. Nationwide there are 3 million cases of child abuse, neglect, or abandonment annually. One church can't make a dent in those numbers. In 1990, I felt the call of God to do this full-time nationwide."

The Tesches knew from experience that franchising is a means of growth when the franchisor lacks sufficient money, skilled people, and time to achieve growth in-house. Diane had helped start and franchise a fast-food concept in the 1970s, and one of Wayne's college friends became one of the nation's largest franchisees for another fast-food chain. That knowledge led the Tesches to believe that the model of franchising could distribute Royal Family Kids' Camps across America. The goal is to have at least one camp in each of the 3,092 U.S. counties.

Wayne started traveling half the year to sell the concept of Royal Family Kids' Camps to churches. Diane wrote the operations manual for the camps drawing upon her food franchisor experiences. She initially hoped to copy guidelines from camping associations but couldn't find anyone that had well-defined systems that are common in franchising.

"Following our system is nonnegotiable. We take on huge liability as do the operators of individual camps," Diane says. "We take the manual back if they don't run the camp up to our standards."

Individual churches sign on to run a camp, which must operate with a ratio of one counselor for every two children. The church pays for background checks and fingerprinting of counselors, who take 12 to 15 hours of training prior to camp every year. They are permitted use of the Royal Family Kids' Camps trademark and logo of a child dressed in royal robes and crown.

Royal Family Kids' Camps teach leaders from each "franchising" church how to communicate the vision to their congregations in order to recruit volunteers and persuade the county child protective services agency to refer children to the camp. They also explain the importance of renting camp facilities no more than one hour away from the church and of raising funds.

"The easiest way to refer to it when explaining to lay people is as franchising," Diane says. "They all understand what that means. They know if you go to a McDonald's in California, Florida, or Germany, you get the same type of hamburger. We need that consistency for Royal Family Kids' Camps to become a household name."

Royal Family Kids' Camps doesn't make its money from fees paid by the franchising churches, other than for training three to five leaders to establish the local program, the way a franchisor provides training to franchisees. The churches must raise money from donations, grants, and their own missions' budgets to support their own camp. The national organization seeks its own donations and grants. For example, Disney Resort gave $10,000.

"It's a community issue," Wayne says. "One out of three women has a background of abuse. Sixty percent of men on death row were abused as children. Eighty percent of prostitutes where sexualized as children. Every four hours some child dies due to abuse.

"In everything we do, we strive to create positive memories for our campers," he adds. "Most of our campers have never celebrated their birthday, so we hold 'Everybody's Birthday Party' at the camps with birthday boxes filled with small presents."

In 2005, 17 new camps opened, bringing the number of Royal Family Kids' Camps to 140 serving 5,100 children in 39 states and four foreign countries. Churches in 23 different denominations run camps. That growth isn't sufficient for Wayne.

"I won't be pleased until we get a camp in all 3,092 counties of America."

18. FRANCHISING ISN'T FOR EVERY COMPANY

Not every business can or should grow using the franchising concept of tapping other people's money, time, and effort.

■ ■ ■

In the early 1990s, Wes Tyler was president of GCS Service, Inc., a Danbury, Connecticut, repairer of restaurant equipment. The company was successful and growing with $50 million in sales and 18 locations around the country. It identified another ten markets that could be equally successful using GCS's systems and brand name. "On an investment of half-a-million dollars, a person could have a $2.5-million-a-year business with 10 percent to 20 percent profit," Wes says. "We needed professional management from the food service industry to run the business. They didn't need to be technically adept. They just needed to work well managing people."

Growth by franchising was booming, so Wes decided to use this method to attract dedicated owner-operators to run the markets into which GCS wanted to grow. That's when Wes learned an expensive lesson that franchising is not for every successful company, even if it has a brand that's been around for 100 years and a system that has been replicated and proven numerous times.

GCS hired an experienced franchise attorney to set up the legal documentation for franchising GCS territories. Wes reorganized his management team to free up a person to supervise and train the franchisees. The company invested more than $200,000 in the legal and management framework and marketing franchises.

"The first thing we encountered was that (potential franchisees) had a hard time making the intellectual leap from managing food service employees to supervising technical workers. One of the best candidates we had decided to stay as part of a larger organization," Wes says. "We also were competing against other franchisors that promised low initial investments. People would look at a printing franchise and knew at the end of the day they could run the copy machine if they couldn't find and keep technicians. We showed prospects the actual profit and loss statements of new branches we opened, and we still couldn't get them to commit."

GCS wanted so much for its franchising effort to work that it finally sold a franchise to a person with strong financial experience who later would scream at customers and not make the necessary investments in the business. One good way to attract customers was to make contracts with manufacturers to do warranty repairs on their equipment. The manufacturers required GCS to invest some money in order to stock parts that it probably wouldn't sell, Wes says, but the repair work also gave GCS referrals for lucrative ongoing work even after the warranty expired. The residual income was much greater than the initial cost of parts. But the sole franchisee wouldn't solicit and commit to such warranty contracts.

"If we had been successful in signing the buyers we wanted, we probably wouldn't have taken the one franchisee we did," Wes says. "In hindsight we realized we would have been better off not selling even one franchise than selling to the one we did. We should have been more discerning."

GCS eventually bought back the franchise and got out of franchising completely. In 1998, the repair service sold to a *Fortune* 500 company. Wes now owns Old Oak Partners, LLC, an Eaton, Connecticut, investment firm and is president of North American Commercial Parts and Services Inc., a holding company for regional repair services in commercial food equipment. Of his foray into franchising Wes says, "The shame of it was that the business was a proven model but franchising it was a complete failure."

SELECTING FRANCHISEES

■ ■ ■

Trade groups and government regulators continually warn franchise buyers to investigate before they invest. Franchisors must do the same before allowing an individual or corporation to become a franchisee. A growing number of franchisors are adopting sophisticated methods for identifying the people who are the right franchisees for their systems. One size does not fit all. Other franchisors are finding certain groups of people, such as military veterans or existing business owners, to be especially fertile hunting grounds for buyers who fit well in franchising.

19. DUE DILIGENCE OF PROSPECTS A MUST FOR FRANCHISORS

Prudence and laws put the onus on franchisors to do
background checks on people who want to buy a franchise.

■ ■ ■

Daryl Dollinger was a Planet Smoothie franchisee with six stores when founder Martin Sprock started looking around for other concepts for the Raving Brands holding company in Atlanta, Georgia. Tex-Mex food was popular so in 2000, they created Moe's Southwest Grill and started franchising in 2001. The fast-casual restaurant concept exploded, opening more than 200 units in four years. Many franchisees opened multiple units and often combined other Raving Brands franchises, such as P.J.'s Coffee and Wine Bar, Doc Green's Gourmet Salads, or Mama Fu's Asian House.

The company always looked over the financials submitted by prospective franchisees, but about 18 months into business, the franchisor became much more deliberate about checking out people before selling them a franchise, Daryl says. "We didn't check from the beginning because it's not cheap to check; it's time consuming. But people lie about their experience and financial status. Today, everyone sues everyone for anything, so we have become a little paranoid as we've grown."

Individuals who are thinking about buying a franchise are continually warned to do their due diligence about the franchisor, to check the financial promises, interview current and former franchisees if possible, and peruse lawsuits. The franchisor should take equal care to check potential franchisees.

"We take our relationship very seriously," he adds. "These people are my friends. They're my business partners. The checks are as important to the people who come in as partners as they are to employees we hire to build the infrastructure." Even after a person buys a franchise, Raving Brands keeps track of financial and management performance because many of them want to open more than one restaurant under one or more of the holding company's restaurant brands. That ongoing relationship gives the franchisor some assurance of franchisees' abilities, but they must perform well with one store before being allowed to buy another, Daryl says.

The integrity of the franchise system is an important reason for franchisors to investigate the backgrounds of franchise buyers. Potential legal problems are another. Federal laws designed to stop bribery and money laundering have long put the onus on franchisors to do everything in their power to verify that their international franchisees are legitimate. The federal Patriot Act was adopted after the September 11, 2001, terrorist attacks. The act put more verification requirements on franchisors to prevent the financing of terrorist activity and money laundering by domestic and foreign criminals. Experts recommend that franchisors have potential franchisees fill out detailed questionnaires about their companies, management biographies, and references and then verify the information. They should look for red flags, such as prior bankruptcies, nondisclosure of prior lawsuits, references that turn out to be nonexistent, and corporate addresses that are mail drops.

"Prospects send us financial information before we ever meet, but we don't look too diligently until we know they're coming," Daryl says. Mindful of privacy laws, Moe's is careful not to spread an applicant's financial records around, but still checks for accuracy.

"We have turned down people, even though they had the money, if something didn't seem too kosher," Daryl says.

20. ATTRACT LIKE-MINDED FRANCHISEES

The franchisor and its franchisees should agree on the methods
for running and marketing the business in order to maximize
success for both.

■ ■ ■

It's a Grind Coffee House in Long Beach, California, strives to differentiate itself in the highly competitive gourmet coffee café industry with
extraordinary service that not only brings customers back repeatedly but
also prompts them to tell all their friends. "We're in the hospitality business; our core ideology is to provide an exceptional experience," says chief
executive Steven Shoeman. "It's not just one element to this. We look for
franchisees who are naturally social to a certain degree, who go out of their
way to service people. It is important that we attract franchisees with like-
minded philosophical alignment."

It's a Grind's first ambassadors for seeking the right franchisees are the
franchise sales staff. They spent four to eight weeks getting to know prospects, explaining It's a Grind's concept, sending the Uniform Franchise
Offering Circular, answering questions, and looking for the desired franchisee attributes. Prospects must take a personality survey developed by
McQuaig Institute of Executive Development in Toronto, Canada. Thousands of companies have used McQuaig's survey in which the subjects
rank words that do or do not describe themselves. When the prospects ar-
rive at It's a Grind headquarters to learn more about the company and franchise opportunity, all key managers are familiar with their scores. "We use
many elements in selecting franchisees," Steve says. "You can't use a single tool, but if the (survey) shows low sociability, then the senior managers
watch for that in the interviews. We are looking for attributes we know they
need to be good franchisees in the IAG system."

It's a Grind turns down 30 percent to 40 percent of prospects, which requires discipline. It's tempting, especially in new franchises, to sell to everyone who meets the financial requirements. But if the two aren't a good
match, the franchisor will be disappointed and the franchisee will be miser-
able, Steve says. "This is one of the toughest (franchise) concepts to realis-

tically visualize beforehand. (Prospects) think it's *Friends* or *Cheers,* he says, referring to two popular television shows. "They think they'll be out front hanging out, but it is a lot of work and expectations are high."

It's a Grind spends a great deal of time during franchisee training on two important parts of the chain's image: hiring the right employees and community involvement. The first is similar to the franchisor's search for the right franchisee. The franchisee must hire outgoing, service-oriented people, and that is easier for franchisees who are outgoing and service oriented, Steve says. The second is an important part of the original idea of husband and wife cofounders Marty Cox and Louise Montgomery to make It's a Grind an integral part of their neighborhoods. Franchisees are expected to do community outreach. "We train them to reach out to community charities, but whether it is cancer support, or dog adoptions, or churches is up to them. They go out and serve coffee at these events." A person who doesn't like networking at community events is less likely to use this marketing and relationship-building technique successfully.

"People can fake behavior for a while, but in a crunch, people revert to their natural behavior," Steve says. "This can be a high-pressure business. It only hurts us and the franchisee to approve him and he's not happy after he opens. The benefit of selling to like-minded franchisees is they are happy, opening sales are higher, and sales increases are higher compared to the year before."

21. BUILD A SYSTEM THAT ATTRACTS FRANCHISEES

It is the franchisor's duty to develop a framework and franchisee network that will attract quality people to buy franchises.

■ ■ ■

When Kevin Cushing was looking for a franchise to buy in 1995, he visited or talked by telephone with at least 25 franchisees for AlphaGraphics, the printing and business communications company in Salt Lake City, Utah. "I was overwhelmed by the caliber of people who were in the system, people who had come out of Proctor & Gamble or Playtex or Coca-

Cola. It was like looking at prestigious universities. People want to become part of the system," he says.

Kevin was no slouch. He had been president of a company that ran 81 fast-food restaurants around the United States. AlphaGraphics' system and franchisees persuaded him to buy a franchise of his own in Minneapolis, Minnesota. Then in 2004, he became the chief executive of the franchisor leading efforts to keep AlphaGraphics as a company top-notch people want to join. "Over the years, I made it a point to seek out the expertise of (franchisees) throughout the world to learn all that I could to build my business profitability," he says. "Even so, as I came into the CEO role, I was blown away by the talent we have across our network that I had not had the chance to meet before."

That caliber of franchisee is no accident, Kevin says. It is a process that builds on itself over time. The franchisor establishes business systems that work over a long period of time, he says. AlphaGraphics asked its franchisees to help rewrite its franchise agreement in 1992, and regularly seeks their feedback about ways to improve the company and its operations. The franchisor provides many opportunities for franchisees to network and learn from each other, including annual conferences, prestige groups for top producers, such as the Gold Circle, and peer groups in which owners act as boards of advisors for each others' franchises. Such efforts strengthen the franchisees, which in turn makes AlphaGraphics more attractive to quality franchise buyers.

"Some of it is self-fulfilling," Kevin says. "We get good franchisees because of the barriers we have to buying an AlphaGraphics franchise: a level of financial resources that tend to indicate that buyers are more skilled, and the requirements for running our system. Those who meet our criteria thrive, and those who don't, go away.

"We try to talk people out of buying a franchise," he adds. "Initially they have excitement about going into business for themselves. They don't see the dirt in the corners, so to speak. So we work hard in our interviews (of prospects) to ask, 'Have you thought about this?' 'Here's something a lot of people struggle with. How would you handle it?'"

As a franchisee as well as franchisor, Kevin appreciates that people are investing their life savings to open a business of their own. "I take it personally. I have bumped my knee on everything these people are going to run into. It's tragic if it doesn't work out. We want to make sure all the conditions for success are in place."

Although making the franchise purchase difficult sounds counterintuitive, it really benefits the franchisor, as well as the new franchisees and prospects who don't buy, Kevin says. "If it isn't a good fit, you are going to have problems down the road, and those problems are harder to fix," he explains. "A workout (of a troubled franchisee) takes a lot of energy out of an organization. It's not worth the pay you get at the beginning. A franchise system is a community of sorts. You had better be committed to building that community."

22. SELLING FRANCHISES TO MILITARY VETERANS

Americans learn discipline and systems in the military, which
make them good candidates for franchisees.

■ ■ ■

Todd Recknagel knows what it takes to be a franchisee. He was named franchisee of the year by Blimpie International and the International Franchise Association before becoming president of Mr. Handyman, LLC, an Ann Arbor, Michigan, franchisor of residential and business repair services. That knowledge as well as appreciation for the sacrifice and service by members of the U.S. military made him eager to participate when the IFA reinstituted its Veterans Transition Franchise Initiative (VetFran) following the terrorist attacks on September 11, 2001.

VetFran was the brainchild of longtime franchising guru Don Dwyer Sr. during the Gulf War in the early 1990s. He persuaded some franchisors to give discounts to buyers who had received honorable discharges from any branch of the U.S. military. VetFran has the support of the U.S. Department of Veterans Affairs and the U.S. Small Business Administration. The project is a way to say thank you to military veterans and a strategy for franchisors to market to highly skilled people. The industry is always looking for ways to identify and attract individuals who can succeed as franchisees. Some franchisors develop psychological tests; some hone their interview questions to help in this identification process. Don Dwyer, a veteran himself, thought the military experience was a meaningful fit for franchising. However, the project waned after Don Dwyer's death in 1994.

Don's daughter, Dina Dwyer-Owens took charge of the new VetFran task force in 2002. "It's mostly a way for franchising to give back to people who are risking their lives for this country," she explains.

Todd agrees. "The number one reason that we're participating is that there is no greater country in the world than America, and the veteran who goes out, puts his life on the line to defend this country, we want to back 100 percent. When they get out of the military, they may have a pension, but might not be cash rich. So there's a reason to give a vet a break."

Mr. Handyman is one of more than 150 franchising companies that have agreed to offer their "best deal" to military veterans, several hundred of whom have taken advantage of a VetFran offer. Mr. Handyman, for example, gives a 25 percent discount off the initial franchising fee.

"Franchisors are always looking for people who don't have a problem following systems," Dina Dwyer-Owens says. "What you find in veterans, especially officers, is that they are very systematic."

Mr. Handyman actively markets the program, Todd says. "We make it pretty clear that (buyers) get a veteran's discount. We advertise in veterans' and military magazines, such as *GI Jobs* magazine. The response has been amazing."

Ten military veterans took advantage of Mr. Handyman's discount offer in the first two years of the revitalized VetFran program.

"VetFran makes obvious sense," Todd says. "We're very, very patriotic, and at the same time we're looking for absolutely the best candidates to start businesses in local marketplaces."

Mr. Handyman seeks franchisees who can manage schedules and people. The franchisees hire people with various plumbing, electrical, and woodworking skills rather than do the repair work themselves. That's why many of the franchisees are former business executives and financial managers.

"When you consider veterans, they make phenomenal candidates for franchising. They tend to be very disciplined individuals," Todd adds. "They know how to work hard. They have a propensity to succeed. It's like they're prequalified to buy one of our franchises. We're tickled pink that so many military are buying Mr. Handyman franchises."

23. THE CONVERSION FRANCHISOR

While most companies sell franchises as start-ups, the concept can offer a level of professionalism to owners of existing independent businesses.

■ ■ ■

The Dwyer Group in Waco, Texas, has built a substantial franchising empire of repair concepts, such as Mr. Rooter and Mr. Electric. In 1993, it added heating and air-conditioning services with the creation of Aire Serv Heating & Air Conditioning, Inc. The franchisor brought business systems to an industry dominated by people with good technical skills. "These are people who are excellent at fixing air conditioners and furnaces but don't know how to manage employees, generate sales, handle the finances, and other aspects of being in business," says Aire Serv president Doyle James. "We're the support mechanism for everything but the technical side of the business. We look at accounting, marketing, generating calls, setting goals.

"We use a coaching format," Doyle says. "Our primary goal is to coach the owner but we also train their employees, technicians, and the people who answer the phone."

Aire Serv has concentrated its franchise marketing to people who already service heaters and air conditioners. Perhaps as many as 90 percent of its franchisees converted an existing business to an Aire Serv franchise.

"A lot of (independent) businesses are successful for a couple of years, then they reach a point at about five years at which they either grow and mature or run out of money and close," Doyle says. "The owners may reach an age or a point that they recognize that something has to change or they'll get out of the business. But they don't have anything to sell because *they* are the business."

By converting to a franchise and establishing professional operating systems and management, these owners acquire control over their businesses, Doyle explains. Some have been in business so long that they are unwilling to change their management style. "People won't change until the pain of change is less than the pain of remaining the same, that is, not making money."

Some conversion franchisees want to change when the second generation of family members comes into the company, and the founder wants them to learn the right way to run a business, Doyle says. Others get worn down and frustrated. "Every business owner goes through cycles, being overwhelmed by the business side of a company and recognizing they have to change or go do something else."

Some potential buyers come to Aire Serv without experience in the heating and air-conditioning industry. They buy an existing independent business and roll it into an Aire Serv franchise, Doyle says. "These are entrepreneurs with money to invest. Taking an existing business that has plenty of calls but isn't profitable can be a better way to go into business than starting from scratch."

The franchisor can be a component in such deals. One Aire Serv franchisee had started a new location with the goal of building to annual revenues of $2 million. When his revenues were just $500,000, he got the opportunity to buy an independent heating and air-conditioning service doing $2.5 million each year but not making any profit. Often, a smaller firm wouldn't attempt such a leap, but with the help of Aire Serv franchisor analysis and other business services, the franchisee negotiated a good deal and quickly increased his business' total revenues to $4 million. It's an example of the franchisor coaching on the business side in a way that benefits both franchisee and the franchise system.

FRANCHISE RELATIONSHIPS
■ ■ ■

Franchising is a partnership that has been compared to a marriage because of the close interdependence of the two parties. As in marriage, the successful franchisors are those who are focused on making the other party successful instead of only asking "What's in it for me?" Early franchising had plenty of examples of unequal contracts that led to increased government regulations. Today many franchisors are accepting independent franchisee advisory groups that negotiate more balanced contracts, encouraging franchisees to help improve the system, and demanding that franchisees continually train for maximum success.

24. A FAIR FRANCHISE AGREEMENT

A successful long-term relationship requires a contract that is reasonable for both franchisor and franchisee.

■ ■ ■

When Mike Leven worked for several hotel industry franchisees in the 1970s and 1980s, he hated the way the franchisors treated him. "I was talked down to, told how to behave, thrown out of one chain in a reorganization. Paying franchise fees to the franchisor was like . . . taxation without representation."

So when he became president of franchisor Days Inn in 1985 with orders to grow the brand, he vowed to treat his franchisees the way he wanted to be treated. Five years later he took the same attitude to the presidency of Holiday Inn Worldwide, one of the largest franchisors in the world. In 1995, he founded U.S. Franchise Systems in Atlanta, Georgia, to franchise Microtel Inns & Suites, Hawthorn Suites, America's Best Inns and Suites, and AmeriSuites, with the notion that the franchise agreements would be different from what had been standard in franchising.

"Franchising by my standard is a benevolent dictatorship; it can't be a democracy. There are standards and other things we have to dictate," Mike says. "Our goal has been to treat franchisees honorably and reasonably, and our franchise agreement reflects that philosophy."

The differences are not merely cosmetic. Many franchisors reserve the right to unilaterally order substantial changes in standards. USFS requires approval by two-thirds of the franchisees. While other systems won't give franchisees an exclusive territory, USFS gives each franchisee an area of protection the size of which is negotiated depending on competition and other issues impacting demand. If a franchisee wants to sell,

USFS charges the buyer $5,000, not the full new-franchisee application fee, which in many systems is more than $50,000. If a hotel has less than 50 percent occupancy after two years of operation, the franchisee can leave the system without paying liquidated damages. Some franchisors would require the failing franchisee to pay all fees for the full length of the contract. The franchisee agreement is written in simple language that is easy to understand.

Certainly, the agreement favors USFS in some ways, and some issues have been modified because of competitive pressures, Mike says. For example, competitors were trying to lure USFS franchisees away because there were not liquidated damages to pay. Now franchisees with successful hotels do have to pay future royalty fees on a graduated scale.

Still, Mike says, "I believe our agreement to be the fairest in the industry, and as testament, it is fast becoming the model for the license agreement of the future. I am proud when competitors copy us."

This approach has hurt USFS in some ways, Mike says. "In the early going, some competitors went after our franchisees because they didn't have to pay liquidated damages. But essentially, we have survived and succeeded."

More important, USFS doesn't have franchisees complaining about encroachment into their territory and has had only one franchisee lawsuit in company history. No relationship, business or personal, is completely trouble-free, Mike says, but at USFS, its problems with franchisees are a minor part of doing business instead of an every day occurrence.

"Yes, we have normal business disagreements, but they are reasons to compromise, not to divorce," he says.

The main reason to take this approach, Mike says, is because it is the right thing to do. "Over time, you expect that the goodwill you engender will give the company long-term success," he says. "When we started we didn't have brand power. In spite of that, we have grown."

25. GIVE FRANCHISEES VALUE FOR THEIR MONEY

The successful franchisor provides so much value that franchisees believe the royalties and fees they pay are reasonable costs of doing business.

■ ■ ■

Ron Berger has had decades of experience building successful franchise and independent companies ranging from a chain of camera stores to video rental stores to specialty sports apparel shop. In 2001, he fulfilled a longtime passion for Manhattan-style pizza restaurants when he and partner Bill LeVine, founder of Postal Instant Press, bought Figaro's Italian Pizza, Inc, pizza chain in Salem, Oregon. Figaro's specializes in pizza baked at the restaurant or taken out in oven-ready trays to bake at home.

Top priority for the franchisor is to provide more than franchisees think they're paying for, he says. "Each franchisor must give value to franchisees. Otherwise you end up with unhappy franchisees. They have to have team spirit so they believe in your system. In terms of royalties, my job as franchisor is to take that money and leverage the combined buying power of all franchisees with services and benefits they couldn't afford on their own."

For example, Ron brought in national operations and buying managers who have worked in some of the nation's largest, most successful franchises. No single franchisee could afford their six-figure salaries. Someone familiar with operations developed over decades at a 1,000-restaurant franchise can avoid mistakes that a small chain might make. Someone who has bought pizza boxes for 1,000 restaurants knows the prices Figaro's should pay. "My job as franchisor is to bring in the best talent money can buy to avoid mistakes, to cause prices to drop across the board," Ron says. "These are the benefits people buy franchises to get."

Although Ron acknowledges that his and Bill's experience in franchising has helped attract industry veterans to Figaro's, "Anyone could do it if he's willing to spend enough money and has a compelling business plan. Some franchisors are not willing to spend the money."

Some franchisors only spend royalty income on building the system, Ron says. At Figaro's, he spends both royalties and initial franchise fees to build a strong infrastructure to create the kind of value he thinks will satisfy franchisees. "You don't have to (spend franchise fees) forever. How many top guys do you need?" he says. "You have to do it until you create critical mass. At some point royalty income is high enough (for the franchisor) to provide value."

Ron bought an existing franchisor to accelerate the growth process he envisioned. Every franchise must have a great concept or food, a great operations manual, great leadership, and great marketing vision, he says. If he started from scratch, he would spend a year developing recipes good enough to franchise. Then he would have to go through the pain of making operational mistakes in order to write procedures to prevent future problems for franchisees. "That's part of what you're paying for as a franchisee," he says. "If they have one store open, good luck. You get a manual with one guy's experience. Figaro's had been around for 21 years when I bought it, and the previous owners had been operations people from Carl's Jr. (regional hamburger chain). I can build the vision immediately."

Within three years, Ron and Bill had doubled the number of Figaro's franchises sold and expanded into 22 states from Oregon to Florida. They anticipate even faster growth through master franchisees in many states.

26. TEAMWORK WITH FRANCHISEES

Franchisees who are encouraged to take active decision-making roles in partnership with the franchisor are more likely to share the passion for building the system.

■ ■ ■

In 1993, after almost ten years as a consultant to the private mail industry and a developer of independent mail and parcel centers, Steven Greenbaum was looking for a means to grow his business, PostNet Postal and Business Services in Henderson, Nevada. He suggested franchising, but his partner Brian Spindel looked at problems encountered by some competitors and questioned whether franchising was really the best vehicle for growth.

"Franchising is a business format that doesn't have to have one certain culture. It can be whatever we want it to be," Greenbaum says. "A franchise must maintain integrity and have standards, controls, and compliance. But how you exercise that can be very different."

In the early 1990s, much of business consulting stressed the influence of empowering employees to improve a corporation. Steven and Brian decided that open communication and franchisee empowerment would work well for PostNet as well.

"Some franchisors establish a parent-child relationship with their franchisees," Steven says. "They say, 'if you don't do things this one way, you're wrong.' We don't believe in that."

From the beginning of the franchise corporation, PostNet created an advisory council of franchisees. Initially Steven appointed members but soon turned over the task to franchisees themselves so that the council would be autonomous from headquarters.

"The members found their involvement and workload was so significant that they created subcommittees for human resources, conventions, marketing, finance, and store-level profitability," Steven says. "At least 50 franchisees are sharing their experiences and skills with PostNet and each other."

The council has clout in strategic decisions about the company. PostNet is a blend of packing and shipping services and printing and copying services. When the company was deciding which technology and equipment to buy, franchisor executives proposed starting with shipping equipment. The franchisee advisory council strongly endorsed copier technology. So the company decided to study both at the same time.

"When you work together for success of the franchise to make the brand stronger, it's hard to be adversarial," Steven says, acknowledging that this teamwork approach does require franchisor leadership to prevent each franchisee from going off and doing his own thing. But at PostNet, empowered franchisees have stepped up to strengthen the brand, not to fall into anarchy.

PostNet has also established numerous ways for franchisees to talk to headquarters executives and each other. The system has an open message board exclusively for PostNet franchisees. They also can phone in or e-mail any suggestions. Headquarters managers visit the stores regularly. Steve attends each region's meeting at least once a year and the PostNet convention, which is attended by 80 percent of the franchisees.

"Having the ability to meet with and physically touch franchise owners is important so they don't feel intimidated to bring any issue to me," he says.

"One of the key things is enabling franchisees t/
themselves. They can get direct support from h
and online and toll-free telephone support. Co
thing, but you need the tools and encourageme

Many of the PostNet franchisees do tak
the communication sharing tools, and it pays o
improve the company, Steven says. "Most of our best ide.
the franchisees."

27. PERSUADE FRANCHISEES TO FOLLOW THE SYSTEM

The basic value of franchising is a proven system for running a
business, yet many franchisees resist following that system.

■ ■ ■

Ray Lamar started making doughnuts as a teenager in the 1930s. After a career as a stockbroker, he returned to his first love, opening LaMar's
Donuts in a converted gas station in Kansas City, Missouri, in 1960. Jay
Leno, host of NBC's *Tonight Show* dubbed Ray the undisputed king of
doughnuts and Hallmark made a doughnut-shaped greeting card in his
honor. LaMar's didn't start franchising until the early 1990s, and mounting
debts forced the sale of the franchisor in 1997. Buyers Ed Hughes and Jack
Irwin brought in as chief executive Anthony Bonelli, who had more than
25 years of experience in such franchises as McDonald's and Blimpie Subs
& Salads, in 2004. During those years as a franchisee, subfranchisor, and
franchisor, his strength was operations. Anthony's hero was Ray Kroc,
founder of McDonald's Corp. who obsessed on creating systems to assure
that every McDonald's in the world would provide the same consistency,
cleanliness, and value. New franchisors often claim that their concept
would be "the next McDonald's."

A franchise company's system is the foundation of its brand and the
core of what it sells to franchisees. It cannot build a strong brand unless everyone executes the system profitably and well. Yet one of the most common difficulties franchisors mention is the franchisee who won't follow

m. "It doesn't make sense," Anthony says. "The system is what
buying. We have been doing this for 40 years and we know what
s, but some don't get it. I spend an awful lot of time in the process be-
e prospects buy to convince them that they don't have to buy a fran-
hise, but if they do buy one, follow the system. If you have a great system
and bad operators, it doesn't work."

After honesty, the willingness to follow LaMar's system is the top trait
Anthony looks for in prospects. To help build a strong franchise network, Anthony is a big fan of the work of Jim Clifton, chief executive of the Gallup
Organization who is best known for creating a metric-based economic model
that is the basis for improving management performance. "You have to find
the right people and put them in the right positions," Anthony says. "If we
don't think they have the talent for franchising, we won't sell to them."

Former military personnel are among the best franchisees because they
are disciplined and understand the value of having standardized methods
for accomplishing a mission, Anthony says. "Franchisees have to have
enough entrepreneurial spirit to own their own business, but they also have
to appreciate the value of the brand and its systems. I can't tell you how
many people I have turned down because they wouldn't make good franchisees. Still, I've made mistakes." He tells of a young, hardworking couple
who had worked in their parents' restaurants, but once they bought the franchise the wife got pregnant and the couple took six vacations in one year.
The franchise struggled until a new buyer took over and made it a success.

The franchisor must set the tone with honesty and frequent communications, Anthony says. "I work so hard on a daily basis to get franchisees
to believe us and for people to believe us, they have to trust us. We don't
lie to them, even about little things. If I say I will call at a certain time, I
do." To foster communications, the franchisor also has monthly advertising meetings for franchisees, feedback from monthly mystery shoppers,
and quarterly operations inspections. "We spend as much time as they need
if they're having trouble with their financials, if food costs are out of line,
or labor costs are out of line," he says. "We try to listen to them because
they are on the front line. They want customers to be happy."

28. COMMUNICATION IS KING

Franchisors and franchisees, as in any good relationship,
depend on strong, continual communication.

■ ■ ■

As president of the board of directors of The Groton Community
School in Groton, Massachusetts, Sharon DiMinico was looking for ways
to raise money for the school without raising tuition. She decided a store
carrying toys and games to stimulate learning through play and creativity
was not only a moneymaker but also a needed venue in retailing. She
didn't merely start one Learning Express store in Acton, Massachusetts, in
1987, but intended from the beginning to grow the concept through franchising. However, these stores require well-trained franchisees who engage their customers, know them by name, and build their Learning
Express into a hub of community activity.

"That kind of culture begins at the top," Sharon says. "I set up this franchise the way I would want to run a store with frequent communication and
close relationships with franchisees. Kids' toys is a relationship business, so
our storeowners need to be able to communicate well with their customers.
It helps their business if they do. I set an example for them."

The communication begins with training for new franchisees. They
spend six to seven weeks at corporate headquarters and their own location
learning not just how to run a business, but how to give their Learning Express a fun and friendly atmosphere with expert staff proficient in providing advice for parents about the most suitable toys for their children.

The franchisor maintains an intranet to which only Learning Express
Inc. franchisees have access. "We maintain the network server here at
headquarters," Sharon says. "We write articles about what's going on in the
toy industry. Every day we give them buying information, new marketing
programs, or information about new vendors. We send e-mails vis-à-vis
the business several times a day, if needed, to keep everyone informed."

No franchisee has ever complained about the volume of e-mails and
information from the franchisor. In fact, some want even more. "The bottom line is that if they have any question at all, (they can) call us directly,"
Sharon says. "We have a very accessible staff at our headquarters. Franchisees have direct-dial access to everyone in this company, including me. I

answer my own phone. They don't abuse it, especially with me. If anything they're too conservative about calling. They think I'm really busy, and yeah, I am but never too busy to help the franchisees."

Learning Express employs regional managers whose job is to provide ongoing training and support for franchisees. Each month Sharon schedules monthly conference calls with storeowners by region. "We get everyone on the phone—(it's) like talking around the kitchen table with people from the buying and marketing departments about product information, with each other about running their businesses," she says. "For an hour, hour-and-a-half they can ask why we added this item to the catalog or how to handle certain situations."

Twice a year, the entire Learning Express network meets together, at the New York Toy Fair and at the national convention for focus groups, workshops, and social time. Sharon also goes around the country to visit each franchisee in person.

The benefit of this continual communication is to build strong relationships and to help franchisees avoid making mistakes or bad decisions in their businesses, Sharon says. Learning Express is successful only if these individual business owners are successful. "It is through their efforts that they do well," she says. "They are working for themselves, not for me."

29. CREATIVE FRANCHISEES IMPROVE THE SYSTEM

Franchisors should embrace innovations made by franchisees
who are closer to the customer and to the operations.

■ ■ ■

Richard Mueller started working for Domino's Pizza, LLC, in the 1960s when it was a small, Michigan franchisor. He dropped out of college to buy a franchise and built his company to 60 Domino's locations in Ohio and Kentucky before selling them to the company and working in corporate headquarters for a while. In 1981, he left the franchisor to start another Domino's franchisee, RPM Pizza LLC in Gulfport, Mississippi, with his brother, Glenn. The brothers have opened 140 stores in four southern states. So when a longtime franchisee like Richard finds something that will improve the pizza business, Domino's listens.

Richard was wandering the aisles at a pizza trade show in the early 1990s, when he spotted a small vendor with a heated bag that could keep pizza at 170 degrees for 30 minutes. Delivering hot pizza had huge implications for RPM, Glenn says. Business increased and drivers got bigger tips. The franchisor allowed RPM to test the product, which the Muellers called Lightning Bag, and when it was a success, Domino's incorporated the idea systemwide, making improvements, finding other vendors, and renaming the bag "Heatwave."

"One of Domino's strengths is its network of 7,000 stores," Glenn says. "We network, share profit statements, estate plans—very personal data—to help each other run our businesses better. If we have a new idea, we can try it. Not every franchisor allows that. A franchise buyer can read the Uniform Franchise Offering Circular (for a company) but how can it tell how well the franchisees work together, how they're allowed to innovate? The buyer ought to ask for examples."

The Muellers aren't the only innovators at Domino's. Another franchisee, Jeff Goddard, created a flat-bottom ladle that scooped the correct amount of sauce and spread it evenly and quickly over a pizza. It was called the Spoodle and helped Jeff win the company's "World's Fastest Pizza Maker Contest" in 1985. Later, another franchisee modified the Spoodle to make pizza even faster.

"We see our franchisees as the experts," says Domino's spokeswoman Dana Harville. "They make pizza every day. We certainly welcome any improvements they suggest." In addition to allowing franchisees to test new ideas, Domino's encourages the practice with such events as the Pie in the Sky new product contest.

The Muellers also dreamed up the lighted sign to set on the delivery car's roof in the 1980s. "Domino's was only in 10 or 12 states, so we didn't have a national brand name," Glenn says. "When we moved into New Orleans we couldn't afford TV advertising, but we needed a way to let people know that we made deliveries."

Car-top signs at that time were heavy and two-sided. The Muellers figured a way to make a "Domino's Pizza Delivers" sign three-sided, lightweight, and easy to install and remove. The sign was lit using an automobile cigarette lighter adaptor. "Wherever the cars with the sign toppers went, sales increased. Plus people like to know who's coming to their door," Glenn says. "Domino's again liked the idea. They have more resources and time to find the best vendors, so now the sign toppers are standard throughout the system. You open a store, you get sign toppers as part of the deal."

30. FRANCHISEE TRAINING IS THE NUMBER ONE PRIORITY

Many people buy franchises because they don't have the tools
or training to run a business. The franchisor's responsibility is
to give them the tools and training to succeed.

■ ■ ■

Rocksolid Granit USA Inc. in Miami, Florida, is the American franchisor for Granite Transformations, which started in Australia as part of a cabinet-refacing program. Franchisees install quarter-inch slabs over existing kitchen and bathroom countertops without demolition. The franchisor has learned that franchisee training—not just in installations but in business management—is the best assurance for success. "If you start them off correctly, you have less to fine-tune later," says Mark Johnson, international chief executive for Granite Transformations. "If the franchisor wants to see a return on its investment, it gives franchisees as much information as it can. From a selfish perspective, we train them and give good follow-through so they are up to speed faster."

Rocksolid Granit brings every franchisee and one or two key employees for a week of training at corporate headquarters. During those five days they cover operations, finance, sales, advertising and promotions, and installations. The amount of knowledge required is overwhelming for many franchisees. Often one partner or a key employee goes through installation training while the other goes through the other topics, Mark says. Sometimes, a franchisee will go through the business training one month and installations the next month.

Mark has found that training is most effective if the second week is spent at the franchisee's location. If franchisees get two weeks training up front, some of it doesn't seem relevant yet, so they act like they are on a vacation. After the site is chosen and the franchisee is to the point of building the back room and showroom displays, Rocksolid Granit sends its trained installers to work with the franchisee and his or her employees to make sure they know how to do the work correctly. The franchisor's installers also evaluate and certify the franchisee's installers.

"Franchisees will gravitate toward the part of the business they're most comfortable in," Mark says. "If they came from a sales background, they want to run the front of the office; if they were cabinetmakers, they do the installation. We want them to be comfortable with the area at which they are weakest and be really good at their strength."

Rocksolid Granit prefers to sell to franchisees who have either a business background or finish-carpentry experience in which they are good at detail work. General contractors often come in with preconceived notions and a history of habits that must be broken in order to get them to follow Rocksolid Granit's system, Mark says.

After a franchise opens, the franchisor follows through with visits to the location, sometimes several times during the first year. "We decide after each visit when the next one will be, depending on the franchisee's need," Mark says. "Sometimes they take off and never look back. Others need more help."

The franchisor has also developed videos on sales techniques and installation, so a franchisee or his employees can review the information again and again.

Good training for franchisees serves another important purpose for the franchisor, Mark adds. "Prospects looking to buy a franchise will go to our current franchisees, and we want them to say it's great. They are more likely to say that if we train them well in the first place so that they're successful."

31. ONGOING FRANCHISEE TRAINING

A franchisor can help its franchisees be more successful with continual assistance and instruction in all aspects of running a business.

■ ■ ■

Steve and Greg Dale ran their own mobile window washing and miniblind cleaning business during the late 1980s when they were young.

Steve's epiphany for business success came when he read *E-Myth Revisited* by Michael Gerber, who used the concept of franchising to stress the importance of developing systems and being the manager, rather than merely being an employee in your own business. "I discovered there is a lot more money in teaching others to run a business than doing it all myself," Steve says.

He established The Dale Group, now located in Mission Viejo, California, to offer low-cost franchises: The Blind Butler Network specializing in miniblind cleaning; The Blind Brokers Network for in-home window covering sales; and The Installers Network for window covering installation. Rather than depend on franchise fees and royalties, The Dale Group would make its money from a small percentage of all blinds and shutters sold through the network. But Steve soon realized that low cost of entry into business would be meaningless if his franchisees didn't learn how to run a business and make it successful. So he looked at ways that he could help them be as successful as he had been when he was a young, independent business owner.

Steve created 13 DVDs on how to run a Blind Broker Network business, covering everything from sales procedures and creation of a presentation book to best use of QuickBooks for financial recordkeeping. "I hired a QuickBooks consultant to create a simple template so my franchisees could see immediately what was going on with their profit and loss statements," Steve says.

Sometimes initial training is overwhelming for new franchisees. So much is squeezed into a few days. When they open their own businesses, they cannot remember much of what was covered. The DVDs provide all the information so a franchisee can review it as many times as necessary.

Steve also created free, voluntary, three-day "boot camps" at corporate headquarters that he gives to reinforce the initial training that franchisees receive and to impart new techniques, explain new products, and answer questions based on real-life issues franchisees encounter with their customers. "They pay their own way here, but we don't charge for the boot camp," he says. "I don't have to be greedy, and no one wins if they don't succeed." Those who attend are most successful, so Steve encourages franchisees to attend boot camp at least once a year.

In 2002, Steve added yet another ongoing training aid, personal business coaching over the telephone with each franchisee. "Everyone follows the same sales strategy. If someone is having trouble, we can ask half a dozen questions and know the problems they have, whether it's getting in the door, or having jobs cancelled. We can troubleshoot their business over the phone in a couple of minutes."

The overall success rate for The Blind Brokers Network for a decade was 78 percent. Of the failures, half never started business after receiving initial training. Once the personal coaching started, the success rate jumped to 90 percent, Steve says. He also sends out e-mail newsletters with more tips and success stories from franchisees. If something works for one, Steve wants everyone to know and possibly try it in their own market. "It's all about training and that never ends for us," he says.

32. TRAIN FOR SALES, NOT JUST MARKETING

The skills and experience of selling should be the focus of ongoing training that a franchisor provides to franchisees and their employees.

■ ■ ■

After graduating from college, Jim Bender accepted an entry-level job with Ziebart, an automotive services and accessories franchisor, and over the next 20 years worked his way up to president of Ziebart North America. Along the way, his most valuable lessons came when he was in charge of sales and training. While the franchising system depends on franchisees doing the selling, the franchisor can provide training to maximize sales performance. Jim discovered that many of Ziebart's franchisees were their own worst enemy when it came to selling. They needed to learn to evaluate their own sales ability and replace themselves with better salespeople when necessary.

Jim had the opportunity to learn the value of sales skills and of hiring the best salespeople firsthand. He ran 27 company-owned Ziebart stores in seven states, in addition to his various jobs within the franchising organization.

While Jim was in charge of sales, Ziebart had a cooperative advertising program with its franchisees. They put in 60 percent of the cost of various advertising campaigns and the franchisor put in 40 percent. The company also put franchisees through a sales training program, yet sales weren't improving, Jim says. "We were training the wrong people. Franchisees were no good at sales. We needed to work with franchisees' employees and to give the franchisees people who were good at sales."

So, Jim developed a program to hire trained salespeople and put them behind the counter at franchisees' stores. Ziebart started headhunting for good salespeople. Jim shut down the cooperative advertising program for a year and put the money into extensive sales training for employees of franchisees who chose to participate. Most of the franchisees joined the program. Ziebart ended its discounting program. The trained salespeople knew how to make sales and to upsell customers without discounting. Sales improved dramatically.

"I hear franchisees complain all the time that everything their home office tells them doesn't work," says Jim, now a Michigan-based consultant with FranchiseBuyer, a franchise broker. "I tell them the first thing they should do is step back and evaluate how effective their sales skills are."

Few people are natural sales whizzes. A salesperson must have the ability to build trust, to listen to what customers are really saying, to identify if the customer has a need strong enough to require a purchase, and to understand what they really mean when they object to a product or price. All of those abilities can be taught, and franchisor trainers help build a stronger system by helping franchisees turn their employees into competent salespeople.

Sales techniques are learned and must be continually reinforced, Jim says. "Any good, qualified salesperson takes a sales course at least two times a year to keep up on new techniques. Any franchisor or franchisee that has a sales staff should find sales training seminars for those employees."

Even though most franchisees ought to pass off the sales tasks to trained employees, Jim likes working with franchisees more than employees. "They have so much more emotion and intelligence invested in the business than an employee. Franchisees are passionate," Jim says.

The smart franchisor helps its franchisees, even those who are the day-to-day operators, to see the big picture, admit that sales aren't their strong suit, and go out and hire or train others to do the selling.

FINANCING

■ ■ ■

Money is the driving force behind franchising. Franchisors need it to grow their companies. Individuals need it to buy franchises. The franchisor brings in franchisees to help capitalize growth, but it soon realizes that franchising itself costs a great deal of money. The undercapitalized franchisor can endanger the system.

One potential strength of franchising is obtaining lower costs for top-quality suppliers through group buying. Sharing the savings helps both franchisors and franchisees.

Some franchisors find it valuable to help people with the financing to buy a franchise, equipment, inventory, or other expenses of business start-up.

33.

GROWTH BY BOOTSTRAPPING

Many franchisors grow by selling franchises because they lack
sufficient capital to expand by other means.

■ ■ ■

When Michael Haith first saw Maui Wowi Hawaiian Coffee & Smoothies in 1997, the seller of fresh fruit smoothies had been a single-location, mom-and-pop operation for 14 years. He bought the company, moved it to his home state of Colorado and considered how to grow it quickly with little money.

"A lot of franchisors are building companies without venture capital or outside money and that is difficult," Michael says. "We bootstrapped this company, which I'll never, ever do again. It's so difficult."

But if a franchisor lacks capital, Maui Wowi is proof that it can grow quickly. It expanded to more than 300 multiunit franchises within its first six years.

"You can't be a franchisor without franchisees, but how are you going to get them without money for marketing?" is the question Michael answered for Maui Wowi.

"The nonnegotiable is that you have to have a working business model," Michael says. "Once you have that, then you have to have either stunning economic numbers (in one unit) or show that you can recreate the model by having three or four units open. When I started, I thought it was so simple. All you gotta do is turn on the lights, put a banana in the blender and push the button. But that's not true. You need to know how to run a business."

Michael had started two other businesses, but had not franchised previously. He sold the first Maui Wowi franchises to friends and associates for $7,500 just to get multiple units and validate the concept. The company had a brief operations manual, small franchise agreement, two employees, and no brand name. The price for a franchise escalated rapidly as the company and brand grew.

"I think one of the dirty little secrets of franchising is that everyone says they screen applicants but initially you're selling franchises to keep the lights on," he says. "If they're willing to write a check, they're in. We can work with weaker franchisees but it requires more focus on our end. When we had (only) six franchisees, we could do that."

The first franchises were near the Greenwood Village, Colorado, headquarters so Michael could nurture owners even if they weren't seasoned franchisees. He was working more than a hundred hours a week, and his wife worked at Maui Wowi too. But by opening a cluster of franchises, Maui Wowi could demonstrate to franchise brokers and consultants that the system was real and growing.

Business brokers played a big role in growing Maui Wowi, he says. But business brokers need to be cultivated and persuaded that a franchise is a good one. They won't risk their reputation on a questionable deal. "They really don't care if a company is well known. They know a big name doesn't equate to good management," Michael says.

Brokers' payment method worked for the cash-strapped Maui Wowi. Brokers take a large portion of the franchise fee, but not until a franchisee actually signs and pays. Although the price is steep—Maui

Wowi paid $1 million to brokers in its first year alone—the up-front costs are low. The method was largely responsible for the six Maui Wowi franchises growing to 66 in 12 months.

"It's wonderful to sell franchises, but it takes time to build infrastructure," Michael says. "I didn't take a salary for three years to put money back into the company."

Franchise sales slowed to 50 or 60 a year while processes, training, management, and technology were built in order to accommodate twice the annual growth again. Buyers committed to three or ten units, which accelerated growth even more.

"If I had my druthers, I absolutely would not bootstrap," Michael says. But I think companies are much stronger when they bootstrap. The owners have commitment and sacrifice."

34. CAPITALIZING FRANCHISE GROWTH

Growth on royalty revenues alone is slower but may allow for building stronger relations with franchisees.

■ ■ ■

Grant Moore always wanted to be an inventor and at any given time had a dozen projects in various stages of development in his home workshop. A friend finally suggested that Grant would never do anything big unless he picked one of his ideas and focused for ten years on fully developing it. The one Grant selected was a drainage system for raised decks that protected the area beneath the deck from rain and snow. He patented the system of drainage channels and in 1993 opened Dry-B-Lo as an independent business to install the structures on residential decks.

"I started hiring crews to do the work and after hiring and firing 20 guys, I realized this wasn't my cup of tea," Grant says. "My buddy suggested selling dealerships, and that became the business model. This was my first experience in this new distribution method, and every time I sold a dealership I tweaked the contract. Eventually my attorney said I was now a franchise because of the royalty structure. I knew there was more value (for the buyer) in a franchise than a dealership and franchising would legitimize my product, so within six months we had produced a franchise package (in 1997). My dealers eventually converted to franchisees."

From the beginning, Grant knew he didn't want huge overhead in the franchising company that would require borrowing, outside investors, or relying on one-time initial franchise fees. He determined to build Dry-B-Lo on royalty income. Borrowing on the expectation of selling many franchises quickly "is like writing a bad check. The stress involved is like having an overdrawn bank account," he says. "I think it is better to grow overhead based on royalty stream."

However, lack of initial capital requires the franchise system to grow more slowly, which runs the risk of allowing competition to get a foothold and take away the first-to-market advantage, Grant says. In some highly competitive industries, such as restaurants, this strategy might be disastrous, but Dry-B-Lo has a niche and is protected by patents.

"I don't want it to sound like we are against aggressive franchise sales, but it doesn't take a lot of people to run a franchising operation if you are efficient and hire key people," Grant says. "I could have gone into debt, hired big guns (to sell franchises), have 300 franchisees by now, and it might have worked out okay, but I was not willing to take that risk.

"Growing at a slower pace isn't all bad. Companies sometimes throw money at a problem and don't solve it, and it comes back to haunt them. Also, if you are dependent on your royalty stream, it forces you to focus on the health of your franchisees. You're going to make sure they are happy, and if they're happy, they will help you sell more franchises. It all fits together."

Although Grant had never worked in a franchise system, he says he has enjoyed most building the personal relationships with Dry-B-Lo franchisees. "It's almost overused these days, but in my personal experience, the relationship with franchisees is critical to success."

Dry-B-Lo grants exclusive territories that will limit the system to about 300 franchisees nationwide. "That's another reason I didn't want overhead so high that at some point I would have to cut back," he says. "Instead, we are adding new programs and products that will build income for franchisees and royalties for us."

35. CAPITAL NEEDS FAR EXCEED EXPECTATIONS

Franchising is not an inexpensive way to grow a company.
Prepare to tap personal and outside resources to set up proper
systems and legal documentation.

■ ■ ■

Victoria Starr bought an illustrated map while vacationing in Aspen, Colorado, in 1987. As an experienced advertising saleswoman for a weekly newspaper and radio station in her home town, Sun Valley, Idaho, Vicki recognized the map as a good business opportunity. She could create an attractive map highlighting attractions of interest in Sun Valley and sell advertising to local businesses. She started Discovery Map with $1,000 and financed the business from her own resources for 12 years, not really developing any grand vision for growth. The business was a means for giving her time and lifestyle flexibility to raise her two children.

In the early 1990s, Vicki recognized that franchising would be the best model for growth. Discovery Map needed a committed person to own the business in each local community in order to develop relationships with business owners who would buy the advertising. An outside sales team would not be able to build strong relationships. But she didn't actively pursue franchising for several years until she started feeling that she needed to grow or find another career. "I didn't have the money to franchise; I was completely naive about how much it would cost," Vicki says. "I thought it would cost a couple of hundred thousand dollars." But the costs were much higher for drawing up the uniform franchise offering circular and other legal documents, protecting all trademarks, preparing correct financial structure, marketing, and the other necessary steps before selling the first franchise.

Vicki sought a financial backer, bringing in a former banker as a business partner who did not have franchising or entrepreneurial experience. He invested some money and made loans to Discovery Map, which Vicki personally guaranteed. The relationship ended poorly, and Vicki spent three years correcting her financial problems. "We had started franchising in 1999 but lost considerable momentum, but I learned all about franchising," she says.

In 2003, Vicki was again the sole owner of Discovery Map. She had exhausted her personal capital, but she dreaded the idea of taking on another financial partner. Out of the blue she received a call from Paul Ruh, a former chief financial officer for a large franchisee, who had seen the Flagstaff, Arizona, Discovery Map and wanted to buy a franchise or invest in the franchising company. Vicki was skeptical, to say the least. "What are the odds you get a call like that?" she says. "He came and looked at the system. He made an offer that seemed too good to be true, so I didn't believe it. I did extensive Internet research, checked his references. I flew down to meet his family."

Paul bought 50 percent ownership of Discovery Map, now headquartered in Anacortes, Washington, guaranteed other loans to grow the franchising, took over financial management of the company, and has been a great angel for the company, Vicki says. "You have to make sure that partners understand the level of risk they are taking. He's an accountant but he's pretty entrepreneurial. I love franchising, but you must be prepared to spend the money and time, and take the risks to do it right."

36. FINDING SUPPLIERS

A franchisor can bring more value to franchisees by negotiating contracts to achieve price advantages with top product and service suppliers.

■ ■ ■

U.S. Lawns in Orlando, Florida, seeks to give its franchisees a competitive edge over individually owned commercial landscaping companies. Certainly a recognized name and systematic management training are helpful. But the company, one of the nation's largest landscape maintenance franchisors owned by a large landscape and golf course developer, uses its size to leverage pricing advantages for its franchisees as well.

"We negotiate purchasing cooperatives through the manufacturers of lawn mowers, chemicals, plant materials, uniforms, and even logos for their vehicles," says Paul Wolbert, vice president of development for U.S. Lawns. These contracts include such brands as Toro, John Deere, LESCO, and XMark mowers, and WESTCO fertilizers. Because of large national contracts, U.S. Lawns can help its franchisees select and buy equipment at the best price possible in the industry.

U.S. Lawns is taking advantage of a plus in franchising: using the combined size of all its franchisees to negotiate price that is better than they could get on their own or their independent counterparts can get. U.S. Lawns does not require its franchisees to buy through the company, even though some franchisors do mandate such purchasing. Sometimes that requirement helps insure quality and consistency. But sometimes it is a profit center for the franchisor, a practice a prospective franchisee should investigate.

Below-market pricing isn't the only item that franchisors strive to improve for its franchisees. They often negotiate delivery requirements, payment terms, or service levels that can enhance the franchisees' competitive advantage even more.

"Service can be more important than price," Paul explains. One of our successful franchisees buys through us for three of his businesses but not the fourth. His supplier is right across the parking lot so he gets excellent service."

When negotiating contracts, U.S. Lawns explores whether the manufacturer has good local dealers in the communities where U.S. Lawns' franchisees are established, Paul says. "We have been approached by companies we thought would be great, but turned out not to be. It depends on their dealer network. We want to find ones with the best local dealers who deliver the best service."

Usually the contracts are written so that as U.S. Lawns grows and its franchisees buy more products or services, the savings automatically increase, Paul says. U.S. Lawns passes those savings on to franchisees.

The franchisees help find the best deals as well, he adds. One franchisee got a great deal on mulch from a company that delivered only in the state of Florida. The supplier put together a program for the same low price for every Florida franchisee who bought during a six-week period in the spring. "If a franchisee in Georgia wanted the deal, he couldn't get it unless he was willing to go to Florida and pick it up," Paul says.

Franchisees always ask for better deals, but sometimes the search isn't worth the potential savings, Paul says. "If I look long enough I might save three cents, but what is my time worth in trying to hunt down a better deal?"

U.S. Lawns' franchisees usually are people eager to run million-dollar companies, not single guys with a lawn mower and an edger. "We work with the franchisee to build budgets, manage to the budget, and manage to their profit-and-loss statement," Paul says. "The co-op buying helps, but it's more than that. It's a mindset. Some franchisees are so focused on 'I have to put two pickles in the center of the bun' that they don't focus on the big picture and the bottom line. That's what we continually work with them to do."

37. SURVIVING BANKRUPTCY

A faltering company must change processes and attitudes in
order to turn around and move toward success.

■ ■ ■

Harry Loyle, an electrical engineer by education, likes the retail photo industry in general and MotoPhoto imaging centers and portrait studios in particular. After owning an independent camera store in New Jersey, he bought a MotoPhoto franchise in 1985, three years after the Dayton, Ohio, company started franchising. "I liked the culture of people, the industry, the idea of not reinventing the wheel, the mentoring. I was in a personal development phase," he says.

Over the years, Harry bought more MotoPhoto franchises until he became area developer of the Northeast. The company was publicly traded at the time, so he became the largest shareholder and sat on the board of directors. MotoPhoto had a well-known brand but most years, the franchisor wasn't profitable. Then the company was hit by what Harry calls the perfect storm. The photo processing industry was undergoing a huge shift toward digital imaging that MotoPhoto didn't embrace. The terrorist attacks on September 11, 2001, severely hurt tourism, travel, and leisure photography, and MotoPhoto lacked the financial resources to change.

"You know that book, *Who Moved My Cheese?*? Well they didn't move our cheese; they kicked it out of the stadium," he says.

In 2002, Harry and five other MotoPhoto area developers engineered a deal in which MotoPhoto Inc. filed for Chapter 11 bankruptcy protection, and they bought the company assets through the newly created, private Moto Franchise Corporation.

Harry says he stepped in because he thought he could fix the system in which he had personally sold 60 franchises. But it was clear much had to change. The MotoPhoto changes included embracing digital imaging,

expanding how customers could get their photos
proving Internet ordering. The structure to ʲ
strengthened to improve information flow. To ᵎ
chisees, it was important to openly share the
a "tell and show" process. "We are extremely ̺
want the culture to be, but then we must be quick to ᵦ
It's a singular vision that a lot of people make happen."

As Harry explained the changes to franchisees, he acknowledgeᵤ,
don't have the only way to run the business; we have the one that works for
us. If you don't want to go there it doesn't make either of us right or wrong."

The number of MotoPhoto franchises declined from about 300 at the
time of bankruptcy to 204. Open communications about the new vision
helped avoid any franchisee lawsuits during this restructuring, Harry says.

"The decline wasn't just us. In five years the number of independent
one-hour photo processing stores dropped from 25,000 to 6,000. It takes a
lot of effort for anyone to stay in this business," Harry says. "I don't think
losing a franchisee is necessarily bad. Having him go away mad is bad. A
franchisor can't guarantee success. What he can guarantee is a substantial
opportunity where others have succeeded before. We facilitate people to
succeed in business who couldn't make it on their own.

"I'm a team kind of guy; I would rather put people first and the money
will follow," he says. "In franchising you get like-minded people together.
My primary driver now is getting the best out of other people. God doesn't
care how many rolls of film we develop. Business is a means for developing people not the end in itself."

---

38. HELP FRANCHISEES OBTAIN FINANCING

A franchisor grows the company faster and with greater strength
if it can work with franchise buyers on financial assistance.

■ ■ ■

Jack Butorac got his first taste of franchising in the mid-1980s with
a small pizza chain in Louisville, Kentucky. The pizza field was so competitive that he didn't stay with the company. That franchisor was Papa

now one of the world's largest pizza chains. "It's clear that pizza is competitive, but the $25 billion segment is wide open when you have good concept and good business model," Jack says.

In 2002, Jack came across another good pizza concept, Marco's Pizza in Toledo, Ohio, and approached the founder Pasquale Giammarco about becoming a partner. Pasquale had owned Marco's Pizza since 1978 and wasn't ready to give up any control, so he suggested that Jack, an experienced marketer, come on board as a consultant to help grow the company. Less than a year later, Pasquale asked Jack to buy the whole company, which he did in January 2004.

"I saw Marco's as the same kind of opportunity as Papa John's," Jack says. "It took us a while to work out a deal. I stopped counting after 72 different financial models."

Jack's concept was to grow from about 130 franchises to more than 500 within five years by bringing in affluent individuals to buy the rights to at least ten units at a time. One value of such a large chain is marketing strength and brand building. Multiple units in a market can better afford various advertising programs. Jack also wanted to provide a financing vehicle, so that these multiunit franchisees would open all ten units quickly, rather than build one, wait for it to become profitable enough to finance the second and so forth. That approach to multiunit franchising growth can be slower than selling one unit at a time, and would not attract the same type of investor who would expect a faster return on investment.

"When I acquired the franchisor, I thought it would be easy to grow," Jack says. "What shocked me was that financial institutions would not lend to someone who had substantial net worth but had not been in the pizza business before. The company had a long history of success and the economics are so strong. It has low investment and low sales break even (point). The return on investment is great."

Jack learned that most financial institutions are not interested in making loans to business start-ups, especially to people without experience in the specific business and industry. Many also won't lend money for restaurants, which have a higher failure rate than businesses as a whole.

Jack needed to find a way to help multiunit franchisees get financing or his growth strategy would be in jeopardy. He found that lenders liked the idea of a loan loss reserve, an account to cover possible franchisee loan defaults, but he didn't want to use the core business as collateral for that reserve. In a separate deal, Jack agreed with an experienced franchise seller to set up a second company for selling Marco's Pizza franchises and retains a percentage of royalties for the life of the franchise agreement. With the kind of growth Jack proposed, the deal could be worth millions of dollars for the franchise selling company. That company would serve as collateral for the franchisee financing. In addition, a major supplier put up a line of credit.

"When we get multiunit operators out there, Marco's will grow rapidly," Jack says. "With qualified investors, it's easy. A lot of people have that kind of money to invest for the return on investment we're offering."

39. PARTNERING ON THE PURCHASE

When a highly skilled buyer cannot meet a franchisor's financial requirements, a partnership can provide a solution.

■ ■ ■

Daniel Bishop was barely out of his teens when he started a commercial janitorial service in Omaha, Nebraska, in 1959. Twenty years later, the cleaning expert noticed the increased demand for residential service among the middle-income families. He continued cleaning offices, and created a separate company, The Maids International, Inc., to take on the residential market. From the start, Dan wanted to sell franchises to build a national organization renowned for a structured, systematic approach to housecleaning. From the time he sold the first franchise in 1980, he has worked to develop partnerships with his franchisees.

"When I first started, I didn't know anything about franchising," Dan says. "I picked up 20 different Uniform Franchise Offering Circulars, and when I read the litigation section it scared me. One company's (disclosure of lawsuits) was thicker than our entire UFOC. I determined that The Maids would stay out of court, work closely with the people, and go the extra mile if the franchise wasn't working."

Dan has always measured every aspect of his business from how much franchisees spend on advertising to the time it takes to clean a house down to the minute. Fairly soon it is apparent whether a franchisee will succeed or need intervention from headquarters to overcome problems. "If the numbers are going the wrong way and they're not responding to our help, we step in very early and say, 'This might not be a good fit. Let's find a buyer for your franchise.'" Dan explains. "You find little or no litigation in our history. It's easier to spend money (buying out an unsuccessful franchisee) than in a lawsuit."

To avoid such situations as much as possible, The Maids has developed measurements and tests for prospective franchisees to identify those most likely to succeed. "We're looking for very good people who can run multiple territories," Dan says, "The industry had the perception that a man would buy a franchise as a cute little business for his wife. My first target was the businessman . . . who would invest $150,000 to $200,000 for an average of five territories." But occasionally, a potential buyer might have the management and marketing skills and experience to run a multiterritory franchise but not the financial wherewithal. "It's critical that they have financial capabilities, but they might not have the whole amount," Dan says. "We are now looking at people who have been in business before, managed service people, fit our profile without enough money to handle the whole cost."

One applicant, for example, had run a chain of hotels, which has similarities to the cleaning business, Dan says. This person had experience on the cleaning side of that enterprise, had hiring and management experience, and a successful track record. The Maids International will now partner with such a buyer in acquiring a multiterritorial franchise.

Dan got the idea from a childhood friend who owned another commercial cleaning business. "He started a number of other locations as separate business partnerships. He got them started, and the partner, who had to put money in, ran the office. I thought that was an interesting concept."

In one case, an established, successful franchisee wanted to sell, so The Maids International, Inc., bought 75 percent of the business and the new buyer bought 25 percent. "Someone is still putting up serious money at 25 percent," Dan says. "They're off to a running start and have the possibility to grow two ways: acquire more interest in that franchise as they go or add more territories."

This alternative to pure company-owned or franchisee-owned businesses lessens the risk for the buyer and provides The Maids with motivated, skilled managers. It also provides another exit strategy for current franchise owners. The Maids is likely to use this approach for a relatively small number of locations, perhaps 10 percent, Dan says.

GROWTH

■ ■ ■

The purpose of franchising is to grow a company. But the system must be properly structured to support that growth. If the foundation and infrastructure are weak or incomplete, a franchisor might be building a house of cards that will collapse at some point. While growing, the franchisor must make sure its quality and brand remain strong. If problems occur, it is better to slow the growth and adjust. Growth for growth's sake is unwise. It is better to select the right places for growth, domestically and abroad, that the franchisor can support. The franchisor also must factor in surprises that can affect growth.

40. POSITION FOR GROWTH

Create a rules-based company prior to selling franchises.

■ ■ ■

The Book Barn, a used-book store started in Joplin, Missouri, in 1980, evolved into a one-stop shop called Vintage Stock to sell previously owned videogames, music CDs, VHS movies, comic books, posters, toys, and trading cards as well as books.

The partners Rodney Spriggs, Ken Caviness, and Steve Wilcox built Vintage Stock to ten stores in three states. But they lacked the resources to build a larger company, so they decided to grow through franchising, and in 2004 they brought in Craig Slavin, chairman of The Franchise Architects in Bannockburn, Illinois, as a partner of Vintage Stock Franchising Company.

Even longtime, successful businesses might not be ready for franchising, Craig says. "No two projects are alike. Preparing a franchising company is not an assembly line process."

However, Craig maintains that all successful franchising companies ideally have the same elements including operations, organization, technology, legal documentation, sales, financing, human resources, marketing, advertising, branding, and positioning. Furthermore, the company needs to be at the right stage of the growth cycle to bring in specialists to handle those elements.

The first step was creating a rules-based business through its operations and organization. "We had to define, discipline, document, and computerize the business," Craig says. This step included writing operations manuals, preopening manuals, and real estate site selection procedures; creating training programs; and buying a point-of-sale computer system for inventory control. The company wrote its first employee handbook and other human resources materials and created profit sharing programs for employees.

In addition to the point-of-sale system, Vintage Stock needed an intranet for internal communications with franchisees and store managers. It also needed to link store and Web site sales information for financial reports as well as inventory management.

Marketing, advertising, branding, and positioning are related efforts. "They didn't know who their customers were. They just knew everyone from little kids buying videogames to grandmas buying gifts came in the door. But we needed to quantify the market (where they live and why they come in) so we could have some predictive ability in choosing new sites," Craig says.

He brought in experts to design a new logo and signs. They chose new colors for the stores: cobalt blue ceiling, red and lime-green walls, flooring that mimicked airplane rivets. Vintage Stock wants to be an exciting place for people to spend their entertainment dollars. Merchandizing experts came in to rearrange where products were placed: Items that customers willingly make a special trip to buy are now in the back of the store and impulse items are in the front where customers must pass at least twice.

Financially, the company needed to figure out where it made its money. Some product categories like golf trading cards and strategy games were dropped because they weren't profit centers. Some professional sports memorabilia were shifted to Internet sales only because they cost too much for shoppers of retail locations.

"It's not that Vintage Stock is a different business," Craig says. "It's the same business at a different level. We have made the value proposition to the customer and the franchisee greater."

Vintage Stock is growing through the sale of multiunit franchises to people capable of opening three to eight locations. But the franchisor is pacing the number of these franchises it sells.

"You can outsell your ability to build stores," Craig says. "But I became a partner because the company has huge potential."

41. SUPPORT SYSTEMS AND INFRASTRUCTURE

Even a well-established company must have proper infrastructure to support franchisees if it is to grow.

■ ■ ■

Travis Dickey opened the first Dickey's Barbecue Restaurant in Dallas, Texas, in 1941. The entire menu was beef brisket, ham, ribs, potato chips, barbecue beans, and beverages. Travis's sons, Roland Sr. and T.D., took over in 1967, expanding the menu and opening additional locations. But when Dickey's Barbecue started selling franchises in 1994, it needed more than a 53-year history of success. "You have to have infrastructure, good people, and systems," says company vice president Roland Jr. "You have to spend money on these things, and you have to have operations support out in the field."

Because of its long track record and existing restaurants, Dickey's did have much of the infrastructure in place, Roland Jr. says. A good company can start selling franchises, even if every element of the system in not perfect, but the more complete the framework, the better and more quickly the network will develop. In the early years, Dickey's moved slowly into franchising, selling mostly to friends and customers who observed firsthand the money-making potential of Dickey's company-owned restaurants.

"We had franchisees come in with some different ideas to improve the system, but you need a foundation; you must cover all the bases," Roland Jr. says. "In the last couple of years we have gotten more aggressive with franchise growth because we have that system in place."

Franchisees expect to buy a proven system in a profitable business. That system must be more formalized than in an independent company in order to assure each franchisee's success. "You need to provide lots of support," Roland Jr. says, "in operations, construction and site selection, marketing, accounting and financial, and human resources. We provide all the little things that tend to fall through the cracks (such as) employee handbooks."

Many people buy franchises after decades of working in corporate America where they never had to handle such paperwork as an Internal Revenue Service W-4 tax form and other basics that a small-business owner takes for granted, he says. The franchisor must think through the simplest processes and provide answers for new franchisees. Prospects visit corporate headquarters for what many franchisors call "discovery days." At Dickey's, this time involves meeting with every department head and key employee of the franchisor, visiting several restaurants, and listening to detailed explanations of what a Dickey's franchisee can expect in terms of responsibilities and support. "We have high standards, but we also provide support," Roland Jr. says. "If a store isn't meeting sales growth goals, we're out there coaching every day to make sure the restaurant reflects well on our brand and is profitable. If they do well, they will tell others to join the system; if they don't, we have a problem."

Customer impressions are important to Dickey's growth strategy, so the franchisor provides services to help the franchisees make good impressions, he says. The franchisor sends out secret diners to rate the restaurants and quality assurance reports to advise franchisees how their operations rate. Dickey's also provides field operations managers to partner with franchisees in delivering good products and atmosphere. All of these programs would help even nonfranchisee businesses be the best they could be, but they are essential to a company like Dickey's Barbecue Restaurants, Inc., that wants to grow through franchising.

42. STANDARDS VERSUS GROWTH

Don't sacrifice quality standards in order to reach goals for growth.

■ ■ ■

Brian Scudamore had just graduated from high school in 1989 when he decided that collecting junk would be a good summer job. At first he ran the business, which he called the Rubbish Boys, during summer breaks, but by 1993 he was so busy that he dropped out of the University of British Colombia in Vancouver, Canada, to run the business full time. Rubbish Boys continued to grow, and in 1998, Brian got a clear vision that his business would become the Federal Express of the junk industry. He established systems, changed the name to 1-800-GOT-JUNK?, and started selling franchises.

"Rather than raising money from outside sources and losing control, franchising uses other people's money and energy to build the company," Brian says. "It's the ultimate leverage model."

Brian brought to the junk industry cleanliness, high-tech trucks, uniformed drivers, on-time service, and friendly workers. That image depends on the franchisees to sustain in the field. "It was surprising how quickly I got out of the junk business and became the marketing and branding company, and my franchise partners were vital to our success," Brian says. "I realized how important it was to bring in the right partners because we're only as good as our weakest link."

Brian wanted to grow 1-800-GOT-JUNK? quickly and set high goals for the number of franchises he wanted to sell. Initially he sold franchises to some people who didn't work out. Brian started appreciating the importance of skill, ability, and cultural fit. One buyer who didn't work out had previously filed for bankruptcy twice. "We still told ourselves, 'He's a good guy. He'll be okay.' But bankruptcy is a red flag that shouldn't be ignored," Brian says.

Such experiences led Brian to set up a debriefing process for his headquarters staff. If one person believes a prospect is a wrong fit, the sale isn't made. "When we want to grow and set aggressive goals, we sit with a prospect and think 'if we sign this person, we reach our goal.' Now we're not willing to sacrifice our standards to reach the goal," he explains.

In 2005, for example, 1-800-GOT-JUNK? set a goal of 150 franchises sold by its March convention. The company only had 146. "We could have hit 150," Brian says, "but I'd rather miss and have the right franchise partners. We're an accomplishment driven company but it's not worth sacrificing standards."

Those standards include franchisees with focus, faith, and effort, Brian says. 1-800-GOT-JUNK? wants buyers who consider the franchise their primary source of income so they will focus all their effort on building their business. The company wants franchisees who have faith in their ability to grow the business and in the franchisor's system and brand. And the company wants franchisees with a strong work ethic willing to put forth maximum effort. "We don't want someone who expects to work 20 hours a week," Brian says. "Money isn't the commitment; it's their heart."

The company has attracted press coverage, which has brought more prospective buyers. "We go through 2,500 candidates to do 50 deals," Brian says. "We have come to realize that we don't motivate our franchise partners. We recruit motivated people, give them the structure and systems, and they do the rest."

43. SELECT THE RIGHT TERRITORIES FOR EXPANSION

Carefully match your customer demographics with regions or countries when developing a growth plan that can succeed.

■ ■ ■

Julian Gordon had made steel products, such as metal stairs, for the construction industry since 1970. But in the mid-1990s he wanted to find a way to diversify his company, Gordon Industries in South Boston, Massachusetts, and chose his patented easy-to-assemble steel wheelchair ramp to do it. "What the world really wanted was the cheapest ramp you can get, the easiest one to install, and the fastest one to deliver, and that's what we came up with," he says.

Julian spent three years developing and testing a business method to franchise the sale and rental of these ramps through a separate company, American Ramp Systems. American Ramp Systems already had a well-developed sales system in place near its Massachusetts headquarters through medical equipment dealers and needed a fresh territory in which to demonstrate that a franchise could generate enough sales to support the franchisee. The first franchise was finally sold in Ohio. The choice was not haphazard but the conclusion of careful effort to find the right customer demographics yet not extend beyond the franchisor's ability to provide good service to franchisees.

Julian carefully studied demographics of disabled and aging populations that would be the primary people to buy or rent wheelchair ramps.

He concluded that American Ramp Systems will probably have a maximum of 100 franchisees. Only about one in 200 people is wheelchair-bound, either permanently or temporarily. He calculated that each franchise needs a territory with a million people to have enough business. Julian chose Ohio for the first franchise because it had enough population and was within a day's drive of South Boston so he could easily travel to make presentations when needed. Pennsylvania was then chosen for the same reasons.

Also, American Ramp Systems only had a staff of 20 to provide vital support services that franchisees would expect. For example, the franchisor prequalifies sales leads so franchisees don't waste a lot of time on people who cannot afford the ramps. The franchisor also provides marketing help with advertisements and press kits.

"I couldn't stick franchises in Walla Walla, Washington, and service them as well as I could in Ohio.

A third factor that made Ohio and Pennsylvania better for the initial franchises was the housing stock. These states have a large number of homes with entry steps for which a person in a wheelchair would need a substitute ramp. States where most houses have level entries are less in need of ramps. On the other hand, much of New York City's housing has stairs but no room for wheelchair ramps. Another type of housing for which the ramps are in big demand is mobile homes, typically built 30 inches or more off of the ground.

Territories matching the population and housing demographics and that were a relatively close distance to American Ramp Systems headquarters were sold first. Then as the franchisor could add support staff, it expanded its franchise sales farther geographically to Illinois, Tennessee, Maryland, and the Carolinas. Some states, such as Maine and Montana, will continue to be served through medical supply dealers because they don't have enough population to support a franchise.

"We prefer franchises because they are our partners. They raise awareness of our product in the community and they focus only on our product," Julian says. "A dealer has hundreds of products and doesn't concentrate on selling just our ramps."

44.   INTERNATIONAL FRANCHISING

A company should not sacrifice its standards and systems in
order to sell franchises in foreign countries.

■ ■ ■

In 1984, SUBWAY, the submarine sandwich restaurant chain, had been selling franchises for ten of its 19 years in business. Executives hadn't done much strategic thinking about moving into locations outside the United States. When someone from Bahrain in the Middle East asked to buy a franchise, SUBWAY agreed.

"It wasn't a conscious decision or we would have gone first to Canada which is closer, and they speak English," says Don Fertman, director of development who has been with SUBWAY since 1981.

In 1986, Don went to a trade show in England in hopes of selling franchises in that country. "Franchising as a business format was just coming out of the dark ages there and many people still thought of it as a pyramid scheme," he recalls. "I had to start with educating about franchising first. And that is still an issue in some countries today."

SUBWAY continued for a decade with the approach of selling franchises in foreign countries based on requests. The company grew internationally but not spectacularly, Don says. Then SUBWAY changed its mindset toward international sales, recognizing that international development was a significant part of the business and required significant resources including opening offices in Australia, Singapore, Lebanon, and Amsterdam to service different regions of the world. At the same time, the franchisor developed a strategic plan for focusing its international resources. It developed a proprietary system for identifying the best prospects for global expansion, based on market attractiveness and competitive advantage.

"The target countries had a high degree of fast-food development, high gross domestic product, and high income: United Kingdom, France, Germany, Spain, Mexico, Brazil, the Middle East," he explains. "Going into any given country, you have to do advance work and talk to local people to find out if SUBWAY products will fly. You have to be sure of your marketing strategy. You have to be prepared for long-term sacrifices."

On the other hand, a franchisor must not let local attitudes deter it from entering a promising foreign market, Don adds. "So many times we have come up against people who say 'You don't understand; it's different here. You have to change your system or you won't make it.' I heard that at that first trade show in England. Today, our more than 400 stores in the United Kingdom are pretty much like the Subways in the United States."

SUBWAY dropped the approach of selling master franchises to people who knew nothing of the franchisor's way of doing business. SUBWAY applied to its foreign franchises a support system it used in the United States, where it recruits existing franchisees to be area developers who sell franchises and support franchisees.

"A person is recruited from the ranks who understands our system, and our mindset, has been behind the counter with his hands in the tuna fish, and understands the customers," Don says. "And they are from their local area so they know their country and their culture."

SUBWAY selects countries for franchise development in which it will not have to compromise quality and standards, he says. "We tend to make as few adjustments as possible because we don't want to dilute the consistency and integrity of the brand. A sandwich should taste the same whether you buy it in Nicaragua or Croatia. Certainly we do make some adjustments. In India we must focus on vegetarian products. It's pretty amazing how they can make tofu taste like bologna."

International franchising has become an important part of SUBWAY's growth strategy. Today one-third of its stores are outside the United States and by 2020 half will be in international markets.

45. INTERNATIONAL FRANCHISING IN REVERSE

Foreign franchisors who want to tap the lucrative American
market must adapt to cultural and business differences.

■ ■ ■

Australians Liam and Natalie Crowe and Andrew and Lisa Brooke were enthusiastic customers and then franchisees for Bark Busters Home

Dog Training in Australia and then New Zealand. The company provides behavioral therapy and dog obedience training using a holistic approach in the dog's home.

"To take Bark Busters to New Zealand wasn't that different," Liam says. "Both countries are close by and settled by the British."

But the two couples had a thing or two to learn—and modify—when they became the Bark Busters' master franchisor for the United States based in Greenwood Village, Colorado, in 2000.

"When we got here, we had a distinct expansion plan that went by the wayside in a couple of months," Liam says. "After Colorado, we thought we would move into the (surrounding) states. We now push a metro expansion plan for densely populated areas of such states as Illinois, Texas, and California. The company needs clusters of franchisees within a geographic area to build brand recognition without forcing the owner-operators of the home-based franchises to travel too far.

But that wasn't the only adjustment the Australians had to make to adapt Bark Busters to the American market. Just as U.S. franchising companies eye lucrative foreign markets, foreign franchisors see potential profits in returning the favor and entering the U.S. business world. The transition can be difficult. "We had to change our model when we came here," Liam says. "It was a rude awakening. At one stage we were down to $900 in the checking account."

One key change was how the franchises were priced, Liam says. Australian franchisors establish one, all-inclusive price for their franchises. But American franchisors tend to break the price down into segments, such as an initial franchise fee, a training fee, and others.

"Our franchises were selling slowly so we went to the business brokers, and they said we were not competitive in our pricing," Liam recalls. "So we reduced the total cost from $50,000 to $37,500 (since increased), breaking it down into $22,500 for the franchise fee and $15,000 for training fee and sold smaller territories. It made our franchises more marketable." Bark Busters USA also charges a lower royalty than its Australian counterpart, 8 percent versus 13 percent.

The Australians found that trust had to be earned in the United States.

"It took 12 to 18 months to get trust of franchisees because we were young—none of us in headquarters is over 40—selling franchises mostly to people between the ages of 45 and 60."

One of the Bark Buster franchisees did a satisfaction survey of his colleagues and gave it to the Australian franchisors. "It was a blow to our ego. It came down to our egos. Even though we had been successful in other countries, for some people, that didn't translate into success here," Liam says.

The Australians also encountered cultural differences. "Our sense of humor is sarcasm that a lot of Americans don't like," Liam says. "We're laid back and many potential franchise owners are more professional and serious."

Also, even though Americans and Australians both speak English, they don't speak the same language. When Liam trains a dog, he might call for a break by saying "the dog's knackered (pronounced naked)," meaning tired, but he gets a double take from his American trainees.

"We now give prospective franchise owners a glossary of Australian terms," he says. "American franchisors hold discovery days. We call it a walkabout. Even our operations manual is in Australian, and people keep asking, 'what the heck is that.' So we're rewriting it."

Despite the challenges, Liam and his partners have been right about the market potential of the United States. They sold more than 100 franchises in the first five years. A colleague who started the British franchising company about the same time sold 12 franchises in the same time. The franchisor in Australia had 40 franchisees after ten years.

46. MANAGING MULTIPLE BRANDS

One franchising company can grow multiple regional brands by providing efficiencies and purchasing economies.

■ ■ ■

Christopher Swartz grew up in franchising. His family was an owner of Jreck Subs Group Inc. in New York State. After graduating from the University of Syracuse, he bought the company and strengthened operations and the brand, but he had something bigger in mind.

In 1996, Christopher formed Ultimate Franchise Systems Inc. in Heathrow, Florida, to grow through purchases of regional food chains with well established brand names. Among its purchases are Central Park of

America, a nine-state burger franchise founded in 1982; Sobik's Subs, a Florida chain since 1969; and Mountain Mike's Pizza in California since 1978. Instead of changing the restaurants to Jreck Subs, UFSI maintains each chain's décor, menu, and name. It has more than 600 units in 30 states under 13 different franchise companies, mostly food concepts.

"It's hard, almost impossible, for a strong regional brand to grow into a national brand," Christopher says. "I'm more pessimistic than most in the franchise industry. Some of the best franchise operators have 50 to 200 units but they don't have the capital or whatever to take it national. There aren't many buyers of regional chains, so we're a great answer to the original entrepreneur who wants a liquidation plan. Because we're focused on regional chains, there are a lot of good deals out there. Our vision is to take a 50-unit chain and grow it into a 150-unit chain."

The key has been to build UFSI into a manager of franchisors. By eliminating redundant services such as accounting, franchise compliance, marketing, and purchasing, UFSI achieves economies of scale just as it would by opening company-owned stores or selling franchises to just one name. Christopher is the first to acknowledge that this is a difficult model and infrastructure to build.

"We've done 30 transactions in seven years," Christopher says. "No one deal is the same. We're proud of that. There are other consolidators out there but they buy 100 percent of a brand as we did initially. Now UFSI identifies an equity partner—most are multiunit franchisees in that chain—who wouldn't have the money to buy the brand themselves. They start as minority owners but have the ability to grow to the majority position and we would become a passive investor."

Identifying the right equity partner to run each franchisor is important, Christopher says. "It's a real partnership. If they're not culturally in line with what we're doing, we wouldn't go far down the road with them."

This approach to growth by acquisition has yielded faster growth than UFSI could achieve with just one brand, Christopher says. "When we owned 100 percent of the brand, we were getting 10 percent annual revenue growth. With equity partners we're getting 15 percent to 20 percent. It has to do with entrepreneurial spirit."

The acquisitions open growth opportunities for the franchisees and advancement opportunities for their management staff. Franchisees can choose to own several different brands instead of just one. Some put multiple brands in one location to leverage the real estate. Others place them in different locations within the same market. For example, some New York Burrito franchisees also own Obee's Soups, Salads and Subs.

"We're intrigued by our existing franchise base, when they've saturated a market with one brand, they're prime candidates for another brand within the same market," Christopher explains.

47. THE FRANCHISOR ISN'T IN COMPLETE CONTROL

While franchising offers a system of operation, some governmental issues and franchisee decisions are independent of the franchisor's program.

■ ■ ■

Dan White was a marine biologist by education who was tired of working for others as a technical consultant to franchise companies. Realizing that he was happiest when working for himself, he started Rapid Refill Ink in Eugene, Oregon, in 2002 to remanufacture, refill, and sell inkjet and laser toner cartridges. Almost two billion used toner cartridges are thrown into landfills each year. Most could be remanufactured as many as 30 times, which would save businesses money and help extend the life of the world's landfills. Initially Dan wasn't thinking about franchising Rapid Refill Ink, but a few months after he opened the business, a man came in, looked around, and said, "Wow! This is fantastic. Is it a franchise? If it is, I want to buy one."

He brought in renowned franchising law firm Piper Rudnick to draw up the legal paperwork and started selling franchises in 2004. Dan's goal was to sell 25 franchises in the first year. He sold 99 in the first 11 months. The company didn't even advertise; that growth came from word of mouth. "It blindsided us," he says. "We then scrambled to put infrastructure in place to serve that large a system. We had a small team of very dedicated people. It's amazing what people can do when they want to accomplish something worthwhile. We were working a zillion hours a week. We even stopped selling franchises for four to six weeks to revisit our system. One change we made is how we train (franchisees). People learn differently. You have to be able to deliver a message that speaks to different types of learners."

Rapid growth also puts pressure on Rapid Refill Ink's distribution. Each store uses environmentally friendly store fixtures, such as carpeting with 52 percent post-consumer content such as recycled milk cartons, walls made of 100 percent wheat stock, and countertops made from compressed sunflower seeds. The franchisor is working on a centralized distribution location that will be able to ship "store in a box" materials quickly. Rapid Refill Ink has also automated its store planning process, so a new franchisee can provide store dimensions and find out immediately what equipment, furnishings, and initial inventory to buy.

With that level of growth, the franchisor is not in complete control of every aspect of opening franchises, Dan says. Landlords, sign providers, vendors, government agencies, and new franchisees have influence. A franchise buyer might agree at the time of signing the contract to open within 60 days, but then come back and want to open in 30 days, Dan says. "That puts stress on our system. Now we have schedules and time lines that don't give these folks a choice."

The franchisor has even less control over landlord and governmental approvals, Dan says. In one city, the entire city council insists on approving every new business that opens in town. Another city requires every business to have the same style of sign, which makes it difficult for franchisors trying to build a brand that includes a certain look, letter font, and color scheme. Landlords also have sign restrictions, which is why franchisors, like McDonald's, that want to maintain absolute control over brand style want to own their real estate, Dan explains.

In 2005, Dan sold Rapid Refill Ink to a group of franchising veterans. Dan remains as president and owns several stores. "The investors have the experience and we anticipate having infrastructure in place to allow us to open one new franchise a day," he says.

PART 2

FRANCHISEES

■ ■ ■

The desire to run a business runs deep and wide in the United States. Some people just want to be their own boss. Additionally, as big corporations have laid off longtime employees, replaced people with machines, or sent jobs to lower-cost countries; workers have sought a way to make a living that can't be taken from them. If they have never run a business, they often look at franchising as a guided path to success.

If you don't learn anything else from this book, learn this: Franchising is not a guaranteed success. You must be an informed franchise buyer. While the Federal Trade Commission and several states require franchisors to disclose information about a franchise offering, most government agencies do not verify the information. Don't just read the Uniform Franchise Offering Circular, double check its accuracy. Above all, talk with other current and former franchisees of a system before buying. If you are unwilling to put in the time and effort to research a franchise before buying, you will probably be unhappy with the purchase. If you do not take a hard look at the negatives you inevitably uncover in any franchise you research, you are likely to be exploited or disappointed. Pay the money to have an attorney help you understand the franchise contract and protect your rights. You are unlikely to be able to negotiate much change in the contract individually, but look for an agreement that the franchisor has negotiated with its franchisee advisory group.

Understand what you're getting for your money. It is not true that the FTC prohibits franchisors from making earnings claims. The government agency encourages such disclosure, but does require that these claims be accurate and puts such demanding requirements on those claims that many franchisors won't attempt to comply.

nd your responsibilities as a franchisee. If you don't like the
franchise contract, it's better to walk away than think you can
ferently. Once you are part of a franchise system, you are ob-
low the system and to help it succeed. You will probably work
harder than you did as an employee. You will move outside your comfort
zone: If you are uncomfortable building relationships and selling, get over
it; if you never had a head for financial statements, learn. If you won't take
this advice, then don't become a franchisee.

PURCHASING ISSUES

■ ■ ■

A franchise is one of the costliest purchases an individual will make
in a lifetime, yet most buyers spend more time researching the purchase of
a car than of a franchise. Many base their decision on a romanticized idea
of owning their own business or of a particular brand. Owning a franchise
is a serious business and lifestyle decision and should be researched thoroughly. Most important, examine your strengths, career goals, specific
franchise opportunities, and other franchisees. But other decisions will
arise as well. Should you buy into a young, small system? Should you buy
an existing franchise whose owner is leaving and, if so, under what circumstances? Many experienced people love franchising so much that they
switch from being a franchisor to being a franchisee or vice versa. All these
decisions must be informed.

48. IDENTIFY YOUR PASSION

Before buying a franchise, examine your own interests, skills, and
experiences to identify the type of business that is right for you.

■ ■ ■

Looking back, it seems Ellen Radigan's whole life was preparation
to buy a Snappy Auctions franchise in Alexandria, Virginia. But it took her
many years to realize the fit with the eBay consignment service.

Ellen grew up in a family business. Her father owned a moving and
storage company. Occasionally, customers didn't pay, so their stored items
were sold at auction to recoup company costs. "I saw a lot of junk and a lot
of valuable items," she recalls. To sell successfully on eBay, "you have to
have an interest in stuff and know what it's worth."

Although Ellen expected eventually to own a business, she spent years
in corporate America and became skilled in sales for companies like East-
man Kodak and various telecommunications giants. "I wasn't happy, so for
eight or ten years, I kicked around different ideas," Ellen says. "What
would make me happy? It wasn't going to be the corporate world. I thought
about starting a professional woman's clothing store or an event-planning
company. I had an antique store on the side that I didn't run myself, but that
got me involved in collecting and buying on eBay."

In 2004, she started exploring businesses she could start. "I wasn't
keen on buying a franchise. Why should I? I wanted to start my own idea
and then franchise it myself," Ellen says.

But then she honestly evaluated what she really liked to do. She enjoyed doing the work and having hands-on involvement in business. She
liked the day-to-day technical aspects of business. She was good at sales.
She had a trained eye for spotting good bargains to buy for her antiques
store. She liked antiques and chocolate.

That evaluation led her to realize that being a franchisee of the right
business would satisfy her more than running a franchising operation. "I'm
not the entrepreneurial type," she says. "I'm a hard worker and independent.
It takes more than entrepreneurial spirit. You have to want to do the work."

She had tentatively decided to buy a gourmet chocolate franchise and
attended a franchising expo in search of financing. "On the way out the

door I saw the Snappy Auctions exhibit and I knew immediately that it was the right thing for me," Ellen says. "For the first time in my life I knew what was right. I'm into antiques. I'm into buying on eBay. I was getting ready to close the antique store and liquidate the inventory. It was a perfect fit with what I like to do."

She opened a store in Alexandria, Virginia, where customers drop off items that will sell for at least $50 on eBay. That's where Ellen's product knowledge comes in. She evaluates the product's worth, posts it on eBay, handles all aspects of the transaction and shipping, keeps a commission, and gives the rest to the customer.

Her experience convinced her of the value of Snappy Auctions' software system that made listing on eBay efficient and effective. "I beat other auctions because I put up more pictures and better descriptions," Ellen says.

"A lot of people don't think about what they want to do (before choosing a franchise). They think (about) whether it's a good business," Ellen says. "The fact that I could take something that I already enjoyed was important."

49. DEFINE WHAT YOU WANT

Before buying a franchise take a careful look at what type of
business you want to own and work in.

■ ■ ■

Dave Skromme had many years of experience selling fax machines and mainframe computers to businesses, so when he was searching for a franchise to buy, he knew he wanted one that would capitalize on his business-to-business sales skills. He wanted to own a business to avoid the constant roller coaster he had been on with two corporate layoffs during the 1980s.

Dave also had a list of things he didn't want in a franchise. He did not want a business that had to be open nights and weekends. He did not want anything in the food industry where products could spoil. He did not want a business with a great deal of inventory or cash because of the potential problems of internal or external theft. "In some ways my search was a process of elimination," he says.

Such self-examination is important for would-be franchisees. Some tend to look for get-rich-quick ideas, clever concepts, or low franchise costs. For long-term satisfaction, the buyer should be looking for a match with personality, experience, goals, and lifestyle choices.

A friend of Dave's with a similar career background bought a printing franchise, which Dave looked at, but he noticed another factor that he didn't want: smelly inks in the back shop. Then he looked at an affiliated sign company owned by the same franchisor. "It fit my needs: weekdays, business hours, low inventory, no spoilage, no theft problems, a fun and creative environment," Dave says. So he started researching. "I listened to the presentation and toured probably 20 stores. I couldn't understand it. All the franchisees were happy but they weren't making any money. By talking to them I found that the guy selling franchises wasn't telling everything. He wasn't lying but he wasn't telling the whole story."

A further problem was that the nearest location Dave could buy was in San Francisco, 20 miles from his home in San Mateo, California. Commercial rents were sky high in San Francisco plus he would have a killer commute. "I did a sanity check and thought I should talk to some competitors to make sure this was the right franchise for me."

After visiting two FASTSIGNS stores, Dave noticed several differences. "They called themselves the one-day sign and lettering experts, and they actually did that. The other franchise couldn't get anything done in less than a week. Also, the FASTSIGNS franchisees were more professional." Like icing on a cake, Dave was able to buy a FASTSIGNS franchise a mile from his home. He opened his store in 1988.

He is satisfied with his choice even after all these years. About 70 percent of his work is with businesses and the rest is with churches, schools, and property managers. The challenge, he says, is keeping up with the technological changes in computer-aided sign-making equipment and techniques that require continual capital investment in the business. "The franchise agreement doesn't require it, but if I didn't spend the money, I would fall behind and lose business," Dave says.

50. MATCH YOUR STRENGTHS

When selecting a franchise to purchase, don't limit your search
to industries in which you have worked before; consider
transferable strengths and skills.

■ ■ ■

For more than 12 years, Calvin Yu worked in his family's business-to-business technology company in Dayton, Ohio. When his parents retired, Calvin remained with the business for 18 months to help with the transition. Although he has a college degree in computer science, Calvin wanted to move to Southern California in 2004 and try working in a nontechnical field. He considered looking for a job, but having been a boss and an employee, Calvin decided he wanted to own his own company. "Either way, I always give 110 percent, so in the long haul I might as well work for myself," he says. Calvin investigated buying an independent business, but thought it was financially riskier than he wanted. "In a private business, you're completely on your own," he says. "With a franchise you're not really an entrepreneur. The products and services are laid out for you."

Before investigating franchises to buy, Calvin weighed both his own strengths when he worked in the family business and his long-term goal. "I'm strongest in operations and management," he says. "My five-year goal is to get married, buy a house, and have kids. A franchise is riskier than a job but the potential financial rewards are better."

He wanted to find a franchise that capitalized on his operational strengths, required few employees, and had more reasonable operating hours than restaurants. He intentionally avoided technology franchises and those selling to businesses with which he had prior experience. He wanted experience in a business-to-consumer sector.

Many franchise buyers are most comfortable looking at franchises in industries in which they have prior experience. Some strike out in a completely different field without weighing whether they have any transferable skills to run such a business. Franchising attracts large numbers of former managers and executives who know how to work with employees, write a budget, market, or plan strategically. The most successful franchisees are those who match not just their experience, but their strongest skills to the franchise most in need of those particular skills.

Calvin almost surprised himself that the franchise that rose to the top of his list was Cash Plus Family Financial Service Centers, which provide check cashing, money orders and transfer, and loans of two weeks to a month for people faced with an unexpected expense before payday. He thought about some auto-related franchises because he is passionate about cars, but decided Cash Plus best matched his skills and plan. Calvin bought the rights to the Cash Plus location in Fullerton, California, in 2005.

"What Cash Plus offers is light-years easier to operate than retail and the hours are shorter. Its services are used by a lot of immigrants and middle-income people, and it gives me experience in the consumer sector, which is different from business to business," he explains.

"I intend to open three to five Cash Plus locations and own several different types of businesses," Calvin says. "My ultimate goal is to go back to technology, but experience in other fields with different customer segments will broaden my perspective. Already, my research before buying Cash Plus has opened my eyes to other segments I wouldn't have been aware of previously."

51. RESEARCH BEFORE BUYING

The biggest mistake a franchise buyer can make is not
researching the company and contract before signing the contract.

■ ■ ■

Ken Smith worked in sales for General Electric Medical Systems for 18 years when his brother-in-law, Joe Errico, announced that he was going to start an independent handyman service in Milford, Connecticut. Ken researched the field and discovered that handyman services were growing rapidly, so he decided to bankroll his brother-in-law's business. Soon Joe had all the work he could handle. Ken's son joined the business and soon both men were working every minute but the revenues weren't growing as the trio hoped. "If this business was going to grow, it would have to be through franchising," Ken says. He had another reason for exploring his options. He wanted to join the business. "In the corporate world, things are very fast paced and stressful. They're always looking for double-digit growth and that doesn't come without a price on your health and peace of mind."

So in 2004 Ken started researching again, this time franchises of handyman services. He was determined to learn everything he could before investing tens of thousands of dollars in the initial franchise fee and two to five times more in other start-up costs.

"I researched the various handyman franchises on the Web. I narrowed my choices down to three, based upon their Web content," Ken says. He contacted the three franchise companies and asked for all the documentation they would provide. He read the Uniform Franchise Offering Circular for each and called to ask more questions. Based on that research, he narrowed his research to Handyman Network Inc.

"The franchise business model was built around having a businessman run the franchise, not a contractor," Ken says. "Handyman Network was looking for people like me. If you run a business with sound business principles, you can learn the basics of the operations and do well."

That choice did not end Ken's research. "I attended discovery day at Handyman Network headquarters in Long Beach, California, to confirm my initial opinion of the business model," he says. He also made due-diligence calls to current Handyman Network franchise owners to better understand the business model and economics. "You have to study and listen carefully. No one lied or misled me but they make things seem easier than they are. Business is hard."

Experts always advise would-be franchisees to study the franchisor's disclosure documents and contract and have an attorney knowledgeable about franchising study them as well. The franchisor must disclose such issues as bankruptcies and lawsuits, and this information should not be ignored. Experts recommend talking to as many franchisees as possible, including those who are no longer with the system. Franchisors must give names of current franchisees and any who have left the system within the previous year. Ask current franchisees if they would buy the franchise again.

Ken still would buy a Handyman Network franchise. "It has helped me jump-start my business by a couple of years. We have a large company and multiple support people behind us. A live person answers the phone" through the franchisor's nationwide toll-free phone number.

In addition to franchise owner, Ken also is a "support partner" giving management and sales guidance to six other franchisees in New England. Joe runs the franchise in Milford, Connecticut, and Ken's son expects to buy a territory in the next county.

"The same thing that makes it easy, also can make it difficult, that is following a process," Ken says. "As with most successful businessmen, I believe in myself and my skills to run a business. But since I knew nothing about the handyman business specifically, I decided that it was in my best interest to use a proven business model . . . In almost all cases that I have deviated from the 'program,' I have run into problems."

52. SEEK VALUE, NOT LOWEST PRICE

Don't buy a franchise solely on the basis of price. Shop for quality and earnings potential.

■ ■ ■

Keith and Shelly Hermanson worked at the same company in Billings, Montana. Both jobs required frequent travel and hectic schedules. They had little time for family life. When the company sold and moved away from Montana, the Hermansons decided to look for career opportunities that would give them more control over their time and allow them to remain in Billings.

"We answered an ad in the *Wall Street Journal,* and when they sent us information we found out it was AlphaGraphics, in the printing industry," Shelly says.

The couple spent the next ten months researching their market to determine a type of business that would succeed in Billings. They kept coming back to the print industry. Their banker tried to talk them out of buying a printing business, pointing out that the city of 90,000 population already had 27 printers. "Just what Billings needs, another printer," he said.

Keith says, "We saw it differently. The market was fragmented. A fair number of these shops had a poor product offering. Turnaround time (on orders) was dismal. They had poor customer service and still were able to stay in business. Our decision to start an AlphaGraphics would likely have been different if there was one substantial player with a great professional reputation and exceptional customer service already operating in Billings."

A key factor was AlphaGraphics print shop's focus on business clients, not individuals and its services beyond printing, such as publishing, design, and digital archiving. "We liked the idea of dealing with businesses versus retail customers," Keith says. "Since we had no experience in printing, we felt we needed to partner with someone who could teach us the business like a franchise."

They bought the AlphaGraphics franchise in 1994 even though it wasn't the cheapest of the print franchises. "We researched about a half dozen different printing franchises. The deciding factor was AlphaGraphics had the highest per-store revenue," Keith says. "AlphaGraphics emphasized direct selling as the key . . . the other franchise owners seemed to be a cut above" the competition.

Shelly adds that AlphaGraphics offered a strong support system and a cutting-edge professional look. "When people who have used Alpha-Graphics in other locations move to Billings, they come here because of the excellent customer service they have received in the past."

Shelly, an outgoing person and good networker, handled sales for the franchise. Keith ran operations and management. Still the strong competition in the market made their first year difficult. Then Shelly was diagnosed with cancer. Instead of giving up, the Hermansons focused and eventually built their shop into one of the largest in the AlphaGraphics system with a diverse client base from the medical, finance, education, and law industries. They concentrate on large customers rather than small, marginal jobs, a strategy that is more profitable but demands higher quality work.

"No one customer provides a large percentage of our business," Shelly says. "We don't put all our eggs in one basket."

The Hermansons stress customer service, fast turnaround, and specialties that keep their shop from being perceived as a commodity that can be bought elsewhere for less. They don't sell on price, instead stressing that they may cost a little more but the job will be done right and on time.

"The worst thing you can do is partner with a mediocre company," Keith says. "Don't decide to invest in something simply because you can afford it. It's like buying a $5 stock versus a $100 stock. You may simply own more of something terrible."

53. DON'T BELIEVE THE HYPE

Every franchisor puts the best face on its opportunities.
Franchise buyers must keep reality in mind, not pipe dreams.

■ ■ ■

David Levine had 25 years of marketing, sales, finance, analysis, and systems experience in a wide range of industries when he accompanied a friend to a franchising seminar put on by franchise broker FranNet. Initially, David wanted nothing to do with franchising, thinking of it in terms of nail salons and fast-food restaurants. "But then I decided it didn't hurt to look," he says. "They presented a few different things and Action International was a natural fit for me. Business coaching was what I already did for people."

David bought the franchise to open Action International Business Coaching and Essentials LLC in Highland Park, New Jersey, in 2002. He was the second Action franchisee in New Jersey. It was important, he says, that he bought a franchise that fit his personality and that complemented his skills. Still, it is important for franchisees in any system to be realistic about their expectations, he adds.

"During training they pump you up: You should do X number of clients in X number of months," he says. "They don't make (specific) financial claims but they do say, 'you will do well,' 'you will recoup your investment.' They also told wonderful stories about coaches who signed up clients on their plane ride home from training." In Dan's experience, marketing doesn't go that smoothly

One appeal of franchising is that it offers a proven system for doing business. It can take some of the guess work and trial and error out of the initial phases of starting and running a business. That's helpful for people who might not know what the next step ought to be. "You believe that franchising is a system, and it is," David says. "But you have to work like you're in your own business. Action is a service business. My clientele is buying me rather than the franchisor. That might not be the case with McDonald's but in tons of smaller franchises, the customers are buying the relationship and reputation of the individual franchisee.

"It takes persistence, reputation, and client satisfaction," he adds. "Don't believe their hype."

Action International delivered the services, system, and assistance that it promised, David says, but he is still responsible for building his coaching practice. "We have a network and share our experiences and what works on the (franchisee) intranet. It gives me a sense of belonging while doing my own thing. The Action system, in its favor, is entrepreneurial. They say, 'Here's the system. Go make it better.' Different clients are looking for different styles. If they're looking for a 6-foot-4 blond female, that's not me. My client is buying me, not Action."

David knows that his county has 18,000 companies, each with fewer than 100 employees, whose owners and executives are his most likely clients. He also knows that he doesn't have to work with them all. "I only want ten. I'm already turning business away," he says.

Franchisees in any system need to recognize the natural tension between franchisor and franchisee, David says. The franchisor wants to spend its money attracting more franchisees. The franchisees want help getting leads and more clients. "If they're spending all their money getting more franchisees, they won't be helping you."

54. EVALUATE THE FRANCHISOR'S STABILITY

A franchisee who invests time and money wants assurances that the franchisor will be around to provide support over the long term.

■ ■ ■

After 12 years of working for major staffing companies, Pam Higdon wanted to open her own independent staffing firm. She sought the advice of an industry consultant who had previously owned an independent staffing business. The consultant said if she were to start again she would franchise and recommended Express Personnel Services. Pam didn't buy on that recommendation. She spent 50 to 60 hours researching various staffing franchisors.

Although Pam was confident that she knew the staffing industry, she wanted a franchisor that would provide a quality system and be around in ten years to provide expertise, ongoing training, and hand-holding.

"Because my husband had been active-duty military for 24 ½ years, and we grew up in a small town in Tennessee, we looked for values, integrity, and honesty," Pam says. "Every person (at Express Personnel Services) I dealt with told it to me straight.

"Track record and the quality of the people they hire were important to me," she adds. "For the price I pay (in franchising, start-up, and royalty fees) I'm paying their salaries. I want experts who can enrich the network. When I saw their selection system, marketing materials, and a proven system, I didn't find another that could compare."

Pam and husband, Sam, bought the Durham, North Carolina, Express Personnel Services franchise in 1997. They felt justified in their choice the day the franchise opened. Their computers and grand opening materials were set to ship when UPS went on strike.

"Express put a person on a plane with a bag of materials. They loaned us a programmed computer and shipped things a different way," Pam says. "They went out of their way to do what they promised."

The Higdons bought a second Express Personnel Services franchise in Oxford, North Carolina, in 2001. A month before the office was to open, Pam was diagnosed with a brain aneurism and preparation for brain surgery led to a stroke. The entire Express Personnel Services system was supportive. The franchisor, fellow franchisees, and customers sent 43 bouquets of flowers and 150 get well cards. The Higdons could have backed out of the deal, but decided to go forward because of the strength and stability of the Express Personnel Services system.

"If we needed it, other Express Personnel franchise owners would have come to help us; I've done that for others," Pam says. "We are like a large extended family of former teachers, accountants, production managers, theater actors, former military, human resources people, and engineers. I expect to see that will be true when Express Personnel doubles in size by 2009."

The Higdons were comfortable enough about Express Personnel Service's past support, present growth, and future stability to buy a third franchise in Raleigh, North Carolina, in 2002. Pam says her prepurchase research was as significant a part of their successful choice of a franchise as her experience in the staffing industry.

"It is great to pick something you like or have passion about, but it's a smarter fit to franchise something in the right marketplace with the right franchisor," Pam says. "I encourage others to pick a franchise with her head and not just their heart."

55. BUY AN EXISTING FRANCHISE

An established franchise should bring a customer base and
immediate cash flow.

■ ■ ■

Joy Hofmeister heard that her son's football coach was moving and his wife would have to sell her Kumon Math and Reading Center in Tulsa, Oklahoma. Joy was the mother of four and a teacher by education, so she thought Kumon would be an ideal business for her to buy. Kumon requires its franchisees to be open at least two years before they can sell the business, and this one had been open a year. So in 2001, Joy bought the franchise from the franchisor and the contents from the franchisee. "It was a sweet deal," Joy says. "I was able to build on what someone else did in starting the business. There is a lot of initial groundwork that any business—independent or franchise—has to do. I was able to springboard over that."

The franchisor warned Joy that a change of ownership usually causes many students to leave. So part of her purchase agreement was to work in the center for three months before the sale went through in order to get to know existing students and their parents. She was able to establish relationships so that none of the customers left when she officially took over. In fact, she was able to double the number of students the center was training to more than 100 within six weeks. After six months, she had 180 students and after 30 months, she had more than 300 students. Kumon's business is built primarily by word of mouth from existing students, so Joy obviously did a good job making her first students and their families comfortable with the change of ownership.

Buying an existing franchise gave Joy immediate income and a business with the bugs worked out. She hired more staff than the franchisor recommended so that the center was poised for growth. If parents perceived that teachers had a full load, they wouldn't refer their friends, she reasoned.

In preparing to market, Joy had the franchise's track record to examine so she could determine the type of student and family most likely to stay with Kumon's training program and those most likely to leave. The foundation of an established business also gave her the confidence to make it more difficult for students to enroll so that they would value Kumon's services more highly.

"I had assumed that students were most likely to quit at a level most find hard to do and everyone complains about," Joy says. "But the data said they were leaving one level before that. I also found that if a student stayed with Kumon for a year, they were with us for a lifetime. So I made it hard to enroll. I took the families through a step-by-step process and gave them opportunities not to sign up. Then I made them commit to one year. Parents often ask if all Kumons have that rule. I tell them no and there are five other Kumon centers in Tulsa they can go to, but this is what it would take to be successful."

She first tested the strategy with seventh grade students, which her center's data told her were the most likely to quit Kumon. "If it hadn't worked, I would have changed it," Joy says. "But it worked so I expanded it to every student. People often call and ask how much it costs per hour and I tell them we enroll students annually although they can spread their payments out. It makes them curious because the training isn't what they thought."

56. THE PROS AND CONS OF BEING AN EARLY BUYER

When a franchise is young it lacks brand recognition and market dominance, but it can have greater growth potential than an established company.

■ ■ ■

Ed Udelle and Gerry Cote were working in the business appraisal industry in Palatine, Illinois, and wanted a different type of business to which they could apply their experience in generating high customer service. Ed saw an article in *Fortune* magazine about a young franchisor, 1-800-GOT-JUNK? in Vancouver, British Colombia, that provided clean, professional removal of large amounts of items that people no longer wanted or needed.

"Gerry said, 'You run it and I'll pay for it,'" Ed recalls. "We were the first to open the Chicago market and started when the brand was relatively new."

Being an early franchisee has both blessings and challenges, he says. They have been able to play a positive role in improving the franchise company, which has made their own franchise more valuable. However, profitability has taken longer than it now does for new franchisees.

"Both the franchisor and we were learning as we were going because there was no blueprint on how to build a successful junk removal business," Ed says. "This was an entirely new concept with no clear way to measure market acceptance. As much as others may say what a great idea 1-800-GOT-JUNK? is, thinking of how it may fit in a market and executing its plan are two different things altogether."

When they started in 2001, a territory was a population of one million. They served that entire area with one truck. Within four years, territories were reduced to 125,000 in population and their value has increased tremendously. Ed has sold some territories and added trucks to be able to serve the north and northwest sides of Chicago and adjacent suburbs.

Other partners are serving other areas of the city, and all the nearby franchisees share in marketing, which helps build brand awareness more quickly, Ed says.

"It was extremely difficult at first because we were unknown in our market and the territory was so much larger to get the name out there," he says.

Although 1-800-GOT-JUNK? had a clear vision for how to run the franchises, the rules were less formal in the beginning, Ed says. "We applied a high level of customer service to this franchise that we used in the appraisal business. We provide personal service, follow up with other visits, and lavish customers with candy and cookies. We tightened up the established systems so now it's even more professional than it was at first.

"It's fun, interesting, and different from the appraisal business. Our customer satisfaction is very, very high. The majority of our business is repeat or from referrals. Later franchisees have learned from what we have done."

When Ed and Gerry first started, the brand was unknown and customers thought 1-800-GOT-JUNK? would pay them for their discards. The early franchisees had to educate prospects about the value of having safe, professional, reliable, and clean movers take the material.

Despite annual growth of 30 percent to 40 percent, Ed and Gerry's franchise wasn't profitable for four years. Now that the brand is better established and other franchisees in the region share the financial responsibility for marketing, new franchisees are profitable the first year, Ed says.

"It's a relief that I'm now getting business referrals from other franchisees who had relationships with businesses in my area," he says. "We cross-pollinate each other as well as split the regional advertising costs."

57. BUY THE FRANCHISOR

The franchising relationship is such a unique partnership that
sometimes the franchisees assume leadership of a company.

■ ■ ■

Ed Pendarvis had been the owner and driving force of SUNBELT
Business Brokers since 1983. At first he added offices through partnerships, but in 1993 he started selling franchises. By 2002, SUNBELT had 346
franchises worldwide. Then a group of franchisees heard that a major
banking institution was eying SUNBELT for acquisition and decided to
make a preemptive offer for the franchisor.

When some franchisees first inquired about buying SUNBELT, Ed was
adamant. The company, which he considered his life's work, wasn't for
sale. But the franchisees had a comeback that the outsiders didn't. SUN-
BELT was their life's work too.

Ed agreed to sell the company under the conditions that all franchisees
were eligible to buy stock, that he could buy stock in the new company
named SUNBELT Business Advisors Network, LLC, in Charleston, South
Carolina, and that he would remain chairman for five years. Ed bought 10
percent of the shares and about 85 franchisees bought 90 percent.

The arrangement is not unique. Among the franchisors bought by
groups of their franchisees are Computer Renaissance used technology
equipment retailers, Blimpie sandwich shops, and Coverall Cleaning Concepts commercial cleaning services.

SUNBELT franchisee Steve Thomson in Irvine, California, says he
bought stock because he believes so much in the company and the growth
potential for the business brokerage industry. "I wanted to make sure we
franchisees own the company."

Brian Cross, a franchisee and area developer in Colorado Springs, Colorado, adds that if another company had bought SUNBELT, the corporate
culture would change and likely would not be as understanding of the broker's viewpoint. Ed Pendarvis understood what brokers' lives are like because he had been one his entire career.

Some say the roles of franchisor and franchisee are fundamentally different. One creates and proves the viability of the business concept and the

other runs the system by the book. But most SUNBELT franchisees previously worked in corporate America or in their own businesses, Steve says. "I still consider myself a franchisee, but now I'm also a stockholder in the mother ship."

The franchisees who do own stock don't make a big deal about that difference from nonowner franchisees. When they had their first shareholders meeting to elect a board of directors in Dallas in 2003, they turned around and attended the annual franchisees meeting the next day. They see the big picture of brand development but they also understand firsthand the needs of the franchisees, Steve says. They also have a clearer idea than some franchisors what their individual offices need to succeed. The company has put additional emphasis on broker training and technology development including an enhanced Web site. "Our focus is squarely on services to franchisees, not just on selling more franchises."

Although franchisees own the franchisor, they hired outside professional Michael Auten, with experience at TravelWerx, Carlson Wagonlit Travel, and Holiday Inn International, as chief executive to run the company. SUNBELT has grown under franchisee ownership to almost 400 franchises.

Ed Pendarvis thinks the franchisor benefits by its new ownership arrangement. "The biggest change I see is a much stronger base of ownership, not just financially but in intellectual capacity," he says.

58. FRANCHISOR TO FRANCHISEE

Many people who start working in the franchisor's organization
eventually switch roles in order to buy franchises.

■ ■ ■

Kenneth Franklin's first exposure to franchising was working as a partner with Forrest and Leroy Raffel in the mid-1960s to set up operations for a unique roast beef sandwich fast-food restaurant named Arby's. (Although many people think the name represents the initials for roast beef, it really stands for Raffel Brothers.)

"First I headed up operations, which is a good way to learn the business," Ken says. "Then I became head of franchising. When I sold franchises, I started realizing there is good money to be made as a franchisee."

In 1974, Ken and a longtime friend from Pittsburgh, Pennsylvania, Leon Felman, bought the Arby's franchise in St. Louis, Missouri, building their enterprise to 29 franchised restaurants before selling in 1999.

Being a franchisee "was easy for me because I knew the business so well," Ken says. "I knew the numbers. I knew operations. My partner ran the day to day, which I didn't want to do and I provided money and advice."

Fast-food restaurants have been popular concepts to franchise because the return on investment can be quite high, and costs of operation can be lower than an independent restaurant, Ken says. Even with the initial franchise fee and royalties, the franchisee of a successful restaurant concept sells more than a comparable independent restaurant and benefits from lower cost of supplies and equipment from systemwide buying. Both spend comparable money on advertising, he adds.

"Working as the franchisor first made me a better franchisee because I looked at operations from the franchisor's side," Ken says. "I learned the whole system and (while on the franchisor side) monitored all those operational things. The Arby's system for making roast beef sandwiches was a more complicated system than many restaurants because you have to plan what you're going to make four hours in advance. You'd better know your numbers."

Ken wasn't the only person in Arby's corporate side to become a system franchisee. He even continued working with the corporation until his franchisee company had four restaurants open, and Arby's had become a national franchising chain. Some franchising companies encourage employees and executives in the franchisor organization to become franchisees, preferring to do business with people they know, trust, and train. However, other companies won't allow it, Ken adds, especially if the person wants to work for the franchisor while getting established as a franchisee. "If you're still working for the company and running a franchise that isn't doing well, it's a demotivator for other potential franchise buyers. When I was selling franchises, I had great respect for the person making that investment, giving up a job without other sources of income. I felt a moral, legal, and ethical responsibility to them."

Even as a franchisee, Ken never really left the franchisor part of the equation. He used his experience as a franchisor to start a consulting company, Franchise Developments, Inc. in Pittsburgh to help other companies through the maze of setting up franchise sales.

"I'm really an entrepreneur, and franchisors should avoid selling to entrepreneurs because they're too independent and won't aggressively support the system," Ken says. "I recognized with Arby's that this system worked, so I was comfortable being the franchisee, especially with a partner to run the day-to-day operations. But consulting is my favorite role because of the variety. There's something new every day."

FINANCING

■ ■ ■

Because a franchise is such a major purchase, key financial issues arise. Each franchisee should be attentive to the financial side of the business to assure that the franchisor delivers the promised value and that the individual franchise is making the most of its money. Many franchisees need help making the purchase. Federally guaranteed loans, retirement funds, and financing provided through the franchisor are options for some franchisees.

59.

GET YOUR MONEY'S WORTH

Franchisees should work to ensure that they receive the
promised value from their fees and royalties.

■ ■ ■

After 13 years in the pharmaceutical industry, Ned Berkowitz was tired of traveling all the time. He read an article about the rise of mobile document destruction companies and started exploring opportunities in that industry. He found Canada-based Proshred Security selling franchises. "Having had no personal experience starting and running a business, it appeared to me that growth would be better in a franchise," Ned says. "It had a Web site, marketing materials, and I could say I was part of a bigger system."

In 2002, Ned became the first U.S. Proshred franchisee, setting up business in his Albany, New York, home. "When I started . . . I did everything myself, invoices, sales, drive the truck, keep the books, answer the phones. I had no rent or payroll, but I was only able to grow the business out of cash flow. The franchisor didn't even help me navigate how to get capital."

After about 18 months, Ned was questioning what he was getting for his $35,000 franchise fee and 6.5 percent royalty. "You get to the point that you ask what the true value of a franchise is compared to starting independently."

In 2004, Heron Capital Corp., a franchise management firm in Toronto, Canada, bought the U.S. rights to Proshred Security International. Heron's top officers had been executives in a competing document shredding company and in other franchisors.

"These new guys brought money, experience, and structure to Proshred," Ned says. "They spent more time with us in the first six months than the previous franchisor spent in 18 months."

Heron has retooled the Proshred Web site, negotiated lower-cost equipment leases, a marketing program, online invoice processing, sales training, and an advertising fund. They offer franchisees an online customer relationship management program. They are also imposing higher standards. A franchisee must have an office in a commercial location, an inside sales coordinator, an employee other than the franchisee to drive the truck, and an outside salesperson, Ned says.

If Ned were to buy another franchise, he wouldn't be the first in a system. "I would look at the strength of the brand, the strength of the network," he says. "Now to be able to say 'we service 12 states' brings value to the network by attracting national customers. I will only be as strong as the rest of the network."

He thinks that with his initial experience and capital, he wouldn't have qualified to buy a Proshred franchise under the new standards. "I didn't have the capital requirements. I would tell anyone to absolutely make sure they are well capitalized. If I had started with a quarter-of-a-million dollars and employees, I would be looking to buy my third truck now."

His first month as a franchisee, Ned had $1,700 in sales and built up to between $13,000 and $17,000 a month depending on the season but couldn't push sales higher. Within six months of Heron Capital buying Proshred, Ned's sales topped $25,000 a month.

"Now I'm getting the system and people I thought I was going to get when I first bought the franchise," Ned says. "Just having new blood reinvigorates the company. But they also provide me with more tools to be more effective."

60. WATCH YOUR SPENDING

A franchisee never has unlimited funds, so careful financial
management is a must to build a successful business.

■ ■ ■

Linda Shaw of Charlotte, North Carolina, was laid off after 13 years of handling job quotes for the engineering department of a machine tool company. Her corporate employer had experienced several rounds of layoffs and had become a depressing place to work, so Linda was grateful for the layoff, which included six weeks notice and a severance package. She didn't want another job that would consume her life and lock her into inflexible hours, so she started looking around the Internet for businesses she could run for herself. She bought a KidzArt franchise that offers art instruction to nonartists of all ages. The start-up costs are on the low end of the franchising spectrum with most franchisees running their operations from home and using public or school facilities for many of the classes.

"It's important to proceed methodically," Linda says. "Don't get caught up in buying all the bells and whistles that you think you need, like a fancy office and trendy supplies."

The bootstrap approach to starting a business came naturally to Linda. She and her husband are thrifty by nature. "My mom raised me to survive the next depression," she jokes. "We're conservative about all our spending.

"I follow my brother's advice who had his own business for years. He always said, 'Don't buy pencils until you need a pencil.'"

Linda kept that advice in mind every time she went to an art supply store, which was like a trip to a candy store for artists and art instructors. Before each purchase she asked herself whether she really needed the item to run the business. She has met some franchisees who struggled because they overspent during the start-up phase before revenues came in.

The first-time franchisee should start with some savings, because revenues can take a year or two to build up to cover all living expenses in addition to business costs, marketing, and royalties to the franchisor. The franchisee who doesn't know how to write a budget should ask the franchisor and other franchisees for realistic numbers for expenses and first-year revenues. If the franchisor doesn't offer bookkeeping software, the franchisee ought to buy an inexpensive program such as QuickBooks by Intuit. However, self-discipline is the greatest ally for the franchisee even when the business starts turning a profit. Putting some revenues into savings will help the franchisee weather seasonal fluctuations in income as well as unexpected economic downturns.

"I keep looking at an office space downtown," Linda says. "I sure would like it, but I keep coming back to my brother's advice."

Linda has ten instructors working for her business, which offers classes every day. Her success has prompted her franchisor to ask Linda to mentor other franchisees who are struggling. Money—or the lack of it—is often an issue. So Linda mentioned to KidzArt that many new franchisees lack financial management skills for running a business. "They have now incorporated that into their franchisee training," Linda says.

"You should know your cash flow at all times. If you don't know how to watch and manage your cash flow, there are books out there that tell you how."

61. SBA LOAN FINANCING

Lenders active in the U.S. Small Business Administration's
guaranteed loan program favor franchisees over independents
in making start-up loans.

■ ■ ■

Gerardo and Rosie Barboza were both teachers, but after they were married with a baby on the way, he was looking for a career change. Both liked SUBWAY sandwich shops because they liked the food. At an initial meeting, a SUBWAY representative told the couple that they didn't have to come up with the entire franchise fee and start-up costs. They could finance part of it with a loan guaranteed by the U.S. Small Business Administration. (The SBA does not make direct loans; it merely guarantees a large portion of loans made to qualified businesses by commercial lenders.)

Gerry called 15 lenders to inquire about applying for an SBA loan. The Barbozas found out later that being prequalified for the loan smoothed the way for approval by the franchisor.

Most commercial lenders avoid financing business start-ups. Some won't handle such transactions at all, and others ban certain types of businesses, such as restaurants and dry cleaners, that have the highest failure rates. Still others will finance start-ups only if they are franchises.

"We found it difficult at first," Rosie says. "We didn't have business experience. We had never owned a restaurant. Neither of us had even worked in restaurants. The way we sold ourselves was that we are intelligent people, hardworking, willing to learn, and schooling had taught us to research and implement projects. And we persisted."

The Barbozas also persuaded Comerica Bank-California to make them a loan for the SUBWAY by writing a detailed, 100-page business plan. Again, Gerry read every book on writing a business plan he could find. Although SUBWAY headquarters would not give them financial performance information for its franchise network, some franchisees shared some data. "Then we sat at restaurants and counted customers," Rosie says. "We had been told the average ticket was $6 or $7, so those were the numbers we used. We came pretty close to our actual performance." The business plan wasn't just for the bank. "It helps you cement your ideas about opening the business so you are better prepared to run a business," Rosie says.

The Barbozas combined their savings and a lien on rental property to put up more than the 30 percent required for an SBA loan.

After Comerica Bank preapproved the Barbozas for a franchise loan, they returned to SUBWAY, which had been hesitant to sell them a franchise because of their inexperience. The loan approval helped win the day. They opened their SUBWAY in Moreno Valley, California, in 2002, and paid off the SBA loan within a year. Gerry ran the franchise full time, while Rosie continued her teaching job so they would have a steady income and health benefits while the SUBWAY got established.

The sandwich shop was so successful, the Barbozas wanted to buy a second SUBWAY, but the franchisor wasn't selling any more franchises in their area and there was a waiting list among existing franchisees. So the

Barbozas bought a Maggie Moo's Ice Cream & Treatery franchise about five miles from their SUBWAY shop. "The second SBA loan was much easier to get," Rosie says. "We knew what to expect and collected documentation early on. We knew Comerica would give us the loan, so we checked with another bank just to see if the loan would be better." That bank wouldn't make the loan, even under the SBA program, because it would loan only for certain franchises.

The Barbozas now have two SUBWAYs and two Maggie Moo's in Southern California. "You have to be informed; you can't go in blind," Rosie says. "And you have to be willing to work hard."

62. TAPPING RETIREMENT FUNDS TO BUY A FRANCHISE

When properly structured, a retirement plan rolled over from a previous employer can finance a franchise without penalties and taxes.

■ ■ ■

When Lisa Neyer stopped teaching special education after 30 years, she was too young to retire to inactivity but she wanted a different career. Her husband, Nelson, had years of experience with various franchisors and as an independent consultant with FranChoice helping others find just the right franchise to buy. In 2005, Lisa and Nelson bought a territory in San Clemente, California, for Bark Busters, a dog obedience training service that requires the franchise owner to also operate the business.

Rather than take out a loan or tap regular savings, the Neyers financed the purchase and initial business expenses with a little-known financing method: It is possible to tap into a 401k, individual retirement account, or tax shelter annuity to start or buy a business without income taxes or penalties for withdrawing the money before age 59½. The method—allowed in the federal Employee Retirement Income Security Act of 1974—is marketed under various names, such as Entrepreneur Rollover Stock Ownership Plan or Rainmaker Plan.

The advantage of this method is that the franchisee does not have to make loan payments, which can put pressure on the cash flow of a new franchise. The potential disadvantage is the risk of losing retirement savings. However, if the business fails, the income tax never has to be paid.

Here's how it works: The Neyers created a regular C corporation for their Bark Buster business. Nelson is the president and Lisa is the vice president. The corporation created a self-directed retirement plan and trust account at a bank. Lisa rolled $80,000 from a tax-sheltered annuity into the new corporation's retirement plan. As the plan's trustee, Nelson invested the money to buy shares of the corporation, and the money went into the business bank account and was used for Bark Busters franchise and training fees and other start-up costs of their business called Happy Home Dog Training.

It typically costs about $1,000 to have a specialist set up the plan and create the corporation and about $4,000 to roll over the funds into the new retirement account and get a favorable determination from the Internal Revenue Service that the plan qualifies under federal law. Anyone using this method should get that determination to make sure the plan is set up properly and avoid problems later. It's also a good idea to check with a tax accountant.

"It costs about $800 a year in maintenance fees, but that's about the cost of a financial planner," Nelson says.

Most types of retirement plans can qualify for this financing method, but the franchisee should have at least $30,000 and preferably more, to have enough money for franchising costs and ongoing business expenses for at least a year. The Neyers have other retirement savings and decided against other franchise concepts that would have cost much more than Bark Busters risking more of their old-age pensions than they wanted. Like franchises themselves, this method is no guarantee of success and some people do lose their investment and retirement.

"But it can help a franchise get off the ground," Nelson says. "People who buy a franchise always want to know how long it will take for the business to break even. With a loan, it will take longer, and the business will need to make higher revenues."

As the franchise succeeds and grows, the Neyers can put money back into the retirement plan.

63. FRANCHISOR FINANCING

Some franchisors offer help obtaining capital to buy or run the franchise, which may be the vital incentive to choose that franchise.

■ ■ ■

John Childs was a certified public accountant because his father had been one and he was good with numbers. But accounting wasn't entrepreneurial enough for this risk taker. While reading *Success* magazine in 1997, John saw an advertisement for Aaron's Sales and Lease Ownership for Less franchises for lease-to-own furniture. Aaron's is one of relatively few franchisors who advertise financial results. The Federal Trade Commission encourages such disclosure, but franchisors get into trouble if the numbers are incorrect or cannot be verified. Aaron's bases its claims on its corporate-owned stores. As an accountant, John liked those advertised numbers. "I'm not passionate about furniture or televisions, but I saw the potential," he says. "I looked at other franchises but they didn't have these results and had employee problems."

John sold his accounting practice and bought the area development rights for as many as 12 Aaron's Sales and Lease stores and paid out of his own pocket for the first store in Vancouver, Washington. But he could not even have begun without the franchisor's inventory financing.

A customer might, for example, lease furniture for 24 months but turn it in after a month, and John would then have to sell it as used furniture. "We both lease and sell furniture, but rent-to-own is our main business," John says. "No bank is going to lend money on used furniture. Aaron's guarantees the inventory financing for all its franchisees. I wouldn't be able to get inventory financing any other way. The 5 percent royalty fee I pay is worth it just to get the financing."

Aaron's has been renting furniture since 1955 and owns hundreds of stores in the chain. The franchisor requires its superstores, both corporate-owned and franchised, to have a better selection and lower prices than competitors. That requirement makes inventory the biggest expense for its franchisees. In order to make franchising work for its system; the franchisor assists its franchisees both with proper management of inventory financing and with sources of inventory financing that understand the intricacies of the leasing business. Because of the volume, the lenders make inventory financing convenient and affordable for Aaron's franchisees. "They have a business model that works," John says. "I don't think they have lost money on any leases in all the years they have done this."

Some other franchisors also provide financing or develop relationships with third-party lenders to finance the initial franchise fee, start-up costs, equipment, accounts receivable, or payroll. Aaron's provides only inventory financing. It may be a financial risk for the franchisor, as it is for Aaron's, but this financial assistance is sometimes the incentive that makes the franchise purchase possible.

John says he has been able to get his own real estate loans guaranteed by the U.S. Small Business Administration and lines of credit for growth because the profit margins and cash flow are so good in his stores. "I paid for the first store but haven't had to put in a dime since and I have eight stores," he says.

In his core business, customers acquire furniture or big-screen televisions with Aaron's 90-days-same-as-cash offer. Few customers actually pay off the purchase within 90 days, so the deal converts to a lease. A strong accounts receivable program is a must, John says.

MANAGEMENT
■ ■ ■

Franchising success depends on the day-to-day work of each franchisee. The franchisor can provide the systems, detailed operations manual, marketing, training, and other assistance, but it's up to the franchisee to execute. The advice most frequently offered by current franchisees to those thinking about joining their ranks is to prepare to work hard. Running a business isn't for wimps even if you do have a franchisor's help. The owner-operator confronts leasing decisions, employee issues, government and landlord regulations, and more.

64. NO ESCAPING HARD WORK

Even with a good system, a franchisee still must work hard to
make the business a success.

■ ■ ■

After building a company that manufactured roofing materials to annual sales of $350 million, Tim Moore retired at age 52, expecting never to work again. He was quickly bored. So, he and his brother Michael, a former banker, started looking for a business to buy. "We didn't like the businesses we saw, so we started looking at franchising," Tim says. In 2004, after exploring everything from transmission repair to check-cashing services, the Moores bought a Mr. Handyman, LLC, franchise in Laguna Niguel, California, because it offered the opportunity to bring their professional management experience to a simple but necessary service. They were to run the business, not create handyman jobs for themselves.

"When you work for a big company, like I did for 30 years, you have all these specialists and you only have to worry about your own specialty," Tim says. "When you buy a franchise, you are responsible for everything.

"Business is hard work."

It wasn't that the Mr. Handyman corporate office didn't provide a good system, detailed marketing materials, and plenty of help. "They really are very good, but they can't do everything," Tim says. "We had to go through what you do on every job or business. The first time you do something, it takes longer."

The franchisor provided ads and artwork, but Tim had to figure out the best local places to advertise. "What works in Laguna Niguel may not work in Northern California, let alone in Michigan," Tim says.

The franchisor provided help in setting up the budget, and first-year revenues were right on target. But expenses were 20 percent higher than the standard budget projected because California has much higher costs for office rents and wages than many other parts of the country.

The franchisor provides details about holding a grand opening, security and safety procedures, and field operations. Still it keeps making improvements as the system grows and franchisees provide feedback about their individual experiences, Tim says. Mr. Handyman's franchise owners' council makes recommendations, and the franchisor has listened.

Even with franchisor advice and training, Tim had to figure out how to attract and retain experienced handymen because each local labor market is different. Fortunately, he knew all about human resources from his previous company, and Michael knew bookkeeping and setting up Quick-Books accounting software because of his financial experience. The brothers share the top job, which the franchisor expects one owner to do. They both work 40-hour weeks. A sole franchisee could spend 80 hours.

"I can't even imagine starting this business independently," Tim says. "Mr. Handyman is really good and provides so much support, but any franchisee must expect to work hard."

During his brief retirement, Tim volunteered with SCORE, the nationwide business counseling organization affiliated with the U.S. Small Business Administration. "I did my duty with people who came in with ideas about starting a business," Tim says. "That's when it hit me that most people have no idea how tough it is to start and run a business. It's not the person with the highest intelligence who is the most successful, though that helps. It's the person who gets up the earliest, stays the longest, works nights and weekends, and works the hardest. Franchising doesn't change that part."

65. FOLLOW THE SYSTEM

Franchisees pay a great deal of money for a brand and a proven system of doing business. They ought to use them.

■ ■ ■

After years of working in various management jobs for *Fortune* 500 companies such as PepsiCo, Cedric Ferrell took an executive position with a direct mail company in hopes of earning an ownership position. But he soon realized that his best opportunity to be a business owner was to buy or start his own firm.

"I am a big believer in systems and rules," Cedric says. "One thing that attracted me to franchising was that there was a system already in place. I knew there would be an infrastructure."

He was exploring the purchase of a mail service or copier franchise when he came across The Entrepreneur's Source on the Internet. The Entrepreneur's Source is a franchise broker and consultant that helps would-be business owners explore business opportunities that match their interests, experiences, and financial resources. "I did not set out looking for The Entrepreneur's Source, but following my extensive research, it seemed like a natural fit," Cedric says.

The franchisee is buying a brand and a system for starting and running a specific business that has proved to be successful in other locations. Some franchisors have rigid systems for everything down to the precise placement of two pickles on a hamburger bun. Others are more flexible and encourage franchisees to experiment with new recipes. A service franchise like The Entrepreneur's Source doesn't include equipment, employees, and real estate that are part of the package of restaurants and hotels. In such services, the system for finding customers and providing excellent service becomes even more important. For example, The Entrepreneur's Source trains its franchisees to be career coaches. It supplies a marketing system and materials to manage clients as they explore different opportunities.

"I follow their system as closely as possible," Cedric says. "I acquired the license because I knew that the company had a lot more resources and experience than I did. I have yet to prove these guys (the franchisor) wrong. Why would I want to create my own way of doing things, especially after I paid a lot of money for the franchise?"

The Entrepreneur's Source provides mailings and press releases for its franchisees to send out at specified times of year. Cedric has followed that schedule and received good response as well as press coverage. He has also received business by following the franchisor's recommendation to network at local chambers of commerce and other business organizations. He also is good about following up on every lead that comes through the corporate office. But some franchisees won't do the marketing, and their practices aren't building as quickly as Cedric's.

"There are certain fees that the franchisor recommends that some franchisees aren't comfortable asking for, so they don't but they're not as profitable as a result," Cedric says.

None of the work of business ownership is difficult in the sense of requiring years of technical training, Cedric says. But it does have to be done. And once a franchisor figures out what works, a franchisee ought to at least try it before dismissing it. Franchisees themselves also build the system by suggesting improvements to the system. But those experiments ought not to be at the expense of executing the proven system.

"Some people are too smart for their own good," Cedric says. "They think they know all the answers before asking any questions. Or they're not comfortable doing certain things. They should consider whether they're cut out for ownership."

66. THE IMPORTANCE OF FRANCHISOR SUPPORT

Other than building the brand, support is the most important contribution a franchisor makes to franchisees' success.

■ ■ ■

Eric Holm started his career in restaurants in 1979, as a busboy at a barbecue restaurant. Over the years he owned a number of independent bars and restaurants, including Angel's Diners, which he founded in Orlando, Florida. Eric gained a reputation as a hands-on owner who knew how to do every job in his restaurants, from the kitchen to the executive office. He got to know Golden Corral fresh, grilled steak and all-you-can-eat buffet restaurants because the corporation was an investor in Angel's Diners. After Eric sold that concept to a public company, he became a Golden Corral Buffet & Grill franchisee in Maitland, Florida, in 1997. He named his multiunit company Metro Corral Partners Inc. In 2004, Eric's franchisee company bought fellow Golden Corral franchisee Winston Group in Atlanta, Georgia, making Metro Corral the largest franchisee in the Golden Corral chain. It also owns the top revenue-making restaurants in the system.

"I had 20 years' experience in the restaurant industry by the time I got into franchising, so I was much better equipped than most franchisees," Eric says. "I had worked for Wendy's and McDonald's so I was familiar with the franchise atmosphere. And I knew Golden Corral was a good concept. You can borrow money when you're in a franchised business. As an independent you have to put all your own money into the restaurant."

Despite Eric's long experience in the food service industry, he considers the franchisor's support the most important benefit of a franchise system. "We pay more royalties than any other Golden Corral franchisees," he says. "That's what we pay for: the brand, the system, and the support. In Golden Corral, we get quite a bit of assistance."

Lack of support from the franchisor is the number one complaint of franchisees in various industries nationwide. Their expectations for help range from negotiating real estate leases to answering operational questions quickly to placing enough units in a market to warrant effective regional advertising.

Golden Corral Buffet & Grill treated its restaurant managers as owners even before it got into franchising in 1987. Since then it has seen one of its primary responsibilities to be helping franchisees and those who run the restaurants make money for the system. It provides a marketing program, which Eric augments with his own marketing efforts. Its real estate staff helps franchisees identify the best locations. It provides product research and development and construction expertise.

"The franchisor provides the look, design, process, and marketing; I just have to execute," Eric says. "Golden Corral assigns someone to us to do checkups of our buildings, our marketing. It's the kind of support I expect for my money."

Some franchisors do not provide adequate support to their franchisees, Eric says. Golden Corral, like many franchisors, provides its franchisees a toll-free phone line for questions, franchisee meetings, Internet support, and a franchisee advisory council. But the caliber of the service and personnel involved are as important as the existence of the programs and services, Eric says. Golden Corral Buffet & Grill has good personnel because it promotes experienced, successful managers within its own system and company-owned restaurants. They know the franchise system and the level of assistance they expected when they worked in the restaurants.

67. LOCAL DETAILS FOR THE FRANCHISEE

Even with the most generous franchisor help, the franchisee must handle some particulars that differ from site to site.

■ ■ ■

Barbara and Don MacIsaac's daughter introduced them to franchising. She loved her after-school job at Zpizza in Southern California. After an unpleasant change to a retail job in college, she returned to Zpizza and happiness. The MacIsaacs decided that working together in their own business close to home would be more pleasant than long commutes and long hours working for other people. They sold many of their possession, such as a motor home, and took out a home equity loan in order to open a Zpizza franchise in San Clemente, California, in 2004.

Zpizza headquarters is just a few miles away from the MacIsaacs' location. They were pleased with the training, the continual contact, and assistance with everything from site location to grand opening. But each franchise has unique circumstances that only the franchisee can confront.

The franchisor suggested a couple of locations for the restaurant. But the MacIsaacs had their eye on a new shopping center at a busy intersection with growing residential developments and a large business community nearby.

"We were supposed to be in the first building of this center, but the city made the landlord do a parking study and found the development needed eight more parking spaces. That delayed our opening more than a year," Barbara says. "That was okay because we could save more money, but Don got on a first-name basis with people at city hall working on various approvals." For example, the MacIsaacs bought a quiet, energy efficient hood for the baking area, but it wasn't suitable for cooking with grease. That's fine for Zpizza, which doesn't use grease. But city inspectors, perhaps aware that restaurants come and go, insisted on putting a warning label on the hood that it could not be used with grease.

"There were so many hoops to jump through that are unique to this location. That's why headquarters didn't mention them," Barbara says.

The MacIsaacs got another lesson in dealing with unique circumstances when their cook came into the store two days before the grand opening and announced that the layout was unworkable. There was no work table for making the pizza. The sifter shot flour all over the glass partition through which customers were supposed to be able to watch their food being prepared.

"Architects just don't know the practical application of the layout. What an architect puts on paper is different from the actual work flow," Barbara says. "Before you get your store layout set in stone, have someone look at (the blueprints) who knows about and works in restaurants. Another restaurant is in a long, narrow space with the food cooler at one end and the ovens at the other. It's inefficient."

Despite the unexpected issues, the MacIsaacs are delighted with the family business. Previously, "we could buy what we wanted, go where we wanted, but when you have material things and not each other, what do you really have?" Barbara asks.

The franchisor has since added an attorney to help deal with municipal issues and a general contractor to review new-store layouts for better practicality, but Barbara says they will still bring in their cook and other experienced employees to look over plans before they open their next Zpizza. "Once you have worked in a store, you see these things completely differently," she says.

68. ONE FRANCHISEE AFFECTS THE ENTIRE NETWORK

Although each franchisee is a business owner, his performance and reputation impacts others carrying the same brand name.

■ ■ ■

Ann Marie Hall has spent most of her working career in franchising. After learning the ropes as an employee of a franchisor of convenience stores, she accepted the job as manager of a multiunit FASTSIGNS franchisee in Baltimore, Maryland. Within months, the franchisor of computer-generated, vinyl signage asked Ann Marie if she wanted to buy a seven-month-old franchise in Lancaster, Pennsylvania, 90 minutes away. In 1998, she took over the shop.

"I enjoy merchandizing and selling, so I liked this business," she says. "I was impressed with the relationships, professionalism, and happiness of FASTSIGNS franchisees."

She quadrupled her franchise sales in two years when her husband, Al, retired from the Baltimore police force and joined her in the business. He handles operations and computers. Ann Marie handles sales, marketing, and customer service.

As a top performer for FASTSIGNS in her region, Ann Marie is sensitive to the importance of the performance of all other FASTSIGNS franchisees. "Their business image is not only important for them, but for all the other owners that have the same sign on the front of their building," she says. "If they don't know what they are doing and don't have good management, it creates a bad image for the entire network of franchisees."

She has had new customers move into the area and seek her out, rather than go to a nearer competitor, because they had a good experience and working relationship with a FASTSIGNS store in another state. That's the impact of systemwide quality.

Good franchisees should encourage their franchisor to set performance standards for the entire system and enforce consequences for lack of performance, Ann Marie says. FASTSIGNS has a franchisee advisory council with members from all types of stores, from top performers to average ones. They help the corporation with strategic planning. They also support the franchisor in establishing performance requirements, Ann Marie says. "Every store should be able to accept electronic files from clients, for example. The stores that (cannot) should lose privileges. This franchisor doesn't want to be confrontational (with its franchisees). That's why it's important for (franchise) owners to say 'It's okay to have consequences.'"

FASTSIGNS franchisees want every store in the network to be top quality, Ann Marie says. They want everyone to merchandise their stores to be appealing and to give service that they would expect if they were the customers. "In a lot of cases that doesn't happen in franchising. Some franchisors could say they have 550 shops but that's meaningless if half are (poor quality). You have to make sure when you do your homework that you visit a lot of locations to know that (a particular franchise) has franchisees committed to the same quality you (have)."

Even after her fast start, Ann Marie invested in the most current sign-making technology available. She implemented an aggressive marketing program, and started incentive programs to motivate her workers to provide the best quality work and service.

"That's the mindset of (franchisees) in our network," she says. "We're invested. We have to because technology in this industry forces us to change all the time and invest in improvements. If some franchisees resist change, it hurts the entire FASTSIGNS name."

69. THE VALUE OF A GOOD SITE

Even service franchises need to pay attention to location to
boost business success.

■ ■ ■

Jere and Don Smith were looking for a business that would diversify
their income from her accounting and tax work and his engineering contracts. They wanted something that they could manage, not necessarily do
the day-to-day labor. Jere, especially, wanted to use her MBA degree. In
2004, the couple bought an existing Mr. Transmission franchise in North
Kansas City, Missouri, that was in an excellent location but had faltered
under a previous owner.

The old adage that business success depends on three things: location,
location, location was coined in reference to restaurants and retail shops.
Such factors as high traffic past the location, easy entrance and exit, and
dense population are well-known to the retail sectors. But service businesses like transmission shops have their own set of factors related to location that are important to success, Jere says.

There is a lot of street traffic by our location, which is important," she
says. "People know where we are. They see us all the time."

But individuals can go for years without needing a new transmission on
the family jalopy. So equally important for this Mr. Transmission's success
is its location in an industrial area not far from an airport. Some general repair shops refer their transmission work to the Smiths' Mr. Transmission.
The electric company next door brings its trucks to the Smiths' shop. The
city brings some of its trucks.

"Companies bring us a lot of potential work on their entire fleet of vehicles," Jere says. "That's much more lucrative work than if we were in a
residential area."

However, she notes that the demographics of the surrounding area also
make this location good for Mr. Transmission. It is a mixed income area.
If a community has too high an income profile a transmission shop won't
do as well, she explains, because the residents get new cars every year or
two, long before they need transmission repairs or new transmissions.

"This is a better location for a transmission shop than where we live in the suburbs," Jere says. "I would rather live closer to where I work. This is a 20-minute drive. But because I don't do the transmission work myself, I can work from the home office."

Many franchisors provide assistance in finding a location, but the buyer should independently examine the franchise they are considering purchasing to understand the location factors and demographics most conducive to success. If the site offered isn't right, hold out for a better one.

The neighborhood around the Smiths' Mr. Transmission has a lot of competition from other auto repair shops. Jere considers that a plus because it means there is also a lot of potential work in the area. The franchisor would grant the Smiths an exclusive territory of just three miles' radius. However, to date there are no other Mr. Transmission franchisees within 100 miles. Jere considers this, too, to be a plus. Even though the shop they bought was not a stellar example of customer service, the fact that it had been open since 1987 enhanced the value of the location because people tended to remember that it was there.

"This shop has been the most successful in Kansas City before it was bought and sold a couple of times," Jere says. "We are reestablishing the reputation. We do like the business. Don has turned down some engineering opportunities because he's happy working with the shop."

70. DON'T BE AFRAID TO HIRE

Spend your time on the tasks of highest value and hire others
to maximize the efficiency and profitability of your franchise.

■ ■ ■

When Anne-Marie and Ken Poulin bought a Gotcha Covered franchise for New Smyrna Beach, Florida, in 2003, they thought she would handle the books and Ken would handle sales and installation for the blinds, shades, shutters, and draperies retailer. The first week Ken, who had extensive sales experience at American Express, made several sales. However, after the ordered blinds arrived and he spent the week installing them, revenues dropped dramatically in the following weeks because he hadn't been out selling.

"When we saw the profits we can make on sales, we decided we were paying an expensive installer," Anne-Marie says. "That's when we hired someone else to install blinds so Ken could sell full-time."

Then the couple hired a second and third salesperson, working on commission, and an office assistant to help schedule appointments and installations, receive shipments, and answer telephones.

"When we bought our franchise, most franchisees for Gotcha Covered were one-man teams. They did all the sales and installation and did the bookkeeping when they had time," Anne-Marie says. "They're afraid to hire anyone. They think they can't afford it. But if our salesperson makes a $2,000 sale, the profit is $1,000, and she gets 20 percent, we've made $800 that day. It's a simple concept, but one that's hard for many other franchisees to accept."

One year, the franchisor declared the systemwide theme to be "duplicate yourself" and asked Ken to talk with groups of franchisees about hiring help to grow their businesses.

As the Poulins' business grew, they refined their staffing. An installer who is an employee has no incentive to work quickly; he makes his salary regardless of how many jobs he completes, Ann-Marie says. "So we changed to subcontractors who are paid per blind. They do as much work in a day as our former employee did in a week."

Once business volume grew to support it, they added in-house labor to handle brief follow-up, fix-it visits, because subcontractors charged a minimum of $50 even if the work took two minutes.

The Poulins offered to train their salespeople to be employees, but they realized they could make more money on commission if they hustled. That, too, has helped the Poulins' franchise grow to one of the top sellers in the Gotcha Covered network.

Anne-Marie doesn't think she is skilled at selling, but has strong organizational skills, so at first she managed the office and did QuickBooks. One day, a customer called about draperies. All the salespeople were gone, so Anne-Marie went out on the appointment. "I realized I did well with draperies because it's more creative and less selling," she says. "With blinds, our salespeople are in and out in two hours. With draperies the first appointment is two hours, and then I go back with designs and fabric choices. It's just different from sales, so I have convinced the home office to split the training for selling blinds and draperies."

With some of Anne-Marie's time devoted to drapery sales, the Poulins have hired a second office assistant. They have also trained employees to handle all the tasks the Poulins normally do, so that they can take vacations. "We stay in touch daily with laptop computers and cell phones, but we always used to travel and we want to continue," Ann-Marie says.

71. HARD TO KEEP GOOD HELP

Finding and keeping skilled workers is an ongoing challenge in today's labor market.

■ ■ ■

Franca Sheehy is a teacher who enrolled her own children in a Kumon Math and Reading Center when they lived in Houston, Texas. She was so pleased with the training that when her family moved to Pennsylvania, she drove her son to the nearest Kumon Center in Delaware. However, when the Sheehys moved to Fayetteville, Georgia, the only Kumon Center closed, so Franca decided to open one herself in 1997. "I saw the franchise as a way to make a living that was commensurate with my present career, yet it afforded more flexibility and the potential for a better income," she says. "The most difficult aspect of franchising for me has been the management of personnel. It has been very difficult to get and keep the perfect people for the positions that I need covered (because) it is part-time work."

Staffing issues are not unique to franchises. Especially when the jobs are part time with no benefits, it is difficult for the small business to fill all positions. Turnover is high, which can be expensive. The cost of recruiting and training new workers is also high in terms of time as well as money. Franca does the student evaluations but wants help to grade the students' work and help with office details. "There is a lot of work behind the scenes," she says. "Even if we are open only a few days a week, I work seven days, especially in the beginning. The business side of Kumon affords me more flexibility than a 9-to-5 job, yet I'm always thinking about the business during my waking hours. It took me a while to get used to this."

Franca tried advertising in local publications but found that applicants were often stay-at-home moms who didn't stay at the job very long. She has used former Kumon students who are still in school and only want to work part time for some spending money. She says the honor students are the most reliable workers. Her other source of good workers, who have become the core of her staff of 20, are retired people who want to work part time to keep active.

"A lot of my staff have children who are off to college and they're looking for something to do. They are very dependable," Franca says. "I try to use word of mouth to find employees. My current employees often recommend people to me, either retired people or friends of students."

As a teacher, Franca initially was uncomfortable with the business side of Kumon. She has had to learn to manage employees. "The most surprising thing I have learned is how some employees will agree to days, hours, job descriptions when being interviewed for the job but will try to maneuver me into their own schedules once hired. I have seen this more often than not. I wasn't used to this kind of manipulation."

She has also found that Kumon requires hands-on management because of the high level of customer service needed to attract and keep students and gain their referrals to other students. "You cannot think that you can hire someone to run the business for you, and sit back and reap financial rewards," she says.

72. WHEN THE WORLD IS YOUR TERRITORY

Some franchise concepts benefit from nonexclusive areas in which to do business.

■ ■ ■

Marcie Olinger worked at major corporations for 20 years, honing skills in product development and project management. When her employer was sold, many people were laid off in 2003, including Marcie. It was the best thing that ever happened to her, she says. "I had always wanted to own a business but could never come up with a million-dollar idea. This gave me the opportunity to find what I wanted. At first I rejected franchising. I thought I was too smart for franchising. I didn't want to have someone tell me what to do. But (before she owned a business) I didn't have a clue how many decisions I have to make in running a business. It's such a relief to have someone else make some of those decisions."

After a year of taking time to reassess what she wanted out of work and then exploring businesses to buy, she bought the Overland Park, Kansas, franchise for The Entrepreneur's Source. The company helps would-be business owners find business opportunities that match their interests, experiences, and financial resources, especially in the franchising field.

Marcie, like all other The Entrepreneur's Source franchisees, does not have an exclusive geographic territory in which she is the only one representing the company to whom potential business buyers can turn. In some systems, franchisees consider the lack of protected territory a negative. Lawsuits have centered on the issue of "encroachment," which involves a franchisor either placing franchisees too close together or using other distribution methods, such as product sales to grocery stores or kiosks in nearby schools that cut into franchisees' sales.

However, the arrangement works well for The Entrepreneur's Source, Marcie says, because of the different nature of the service and its marketing. Many business buyers first find The Entrepreneur's Source corporate headquarters, either through articles or Internet searches. The franchisor refers these inquiries to its franchisees. The referrals would not be equal if they only matched the caller's location with the franchisee who is the nearest geographically, she explains. "Each of us pays a monthly advertising fee. We should get referrals equally."

Marcie's first placement, for example, lived in Michigan. Her work is conducted mostly by telephone or over the Internet, so proximity is not an issue.

Marcie estimates that about half her clients came from the franchisor and half from her own marketing. She has clients living all over the United States.

At the same time, Marcie is not prohibited from finding her own clients in the Overland Park, Kansas, area. She can actively market only in Kansas. When she first opened, she sent letters to all her personal and professional acquaintances informing them of her new work and asking their help in finding clients who needed her service. She is a member of a leads group, a chamber of commerce, and a coalition of professionals in noncompeting industries that presents joint seminars. Two other The Entrepreneur's Source franchisees are located in the vicinity, but instead of fighting each other for clients, they cooperate. "We put on seminars together," Marcie says. "I joined the Olathe chamber, one joined the Overland Park chamber and the other joined the Kansas City, Missouri, chamber. There is so much business and we get more of it by working together."

73. MARRYING A FRANCHISE AND AN INDEPENDENT BUSINESS

A franchise concept can ease the seasonality of an independent business, often tapping the same customers for different products or services throughout the year.

■ ■ ■

Since 1990, Dennis Crede has been doing commercial and residential landscaping and maintenance in Scott Depot, West Virginia. It was an excellent business, but in October, the work slowed down and didn't pick up again until the next spring. Dennis was always looking for ways to grow and to keep good employees. If he let them go during the slow winter, they might not return when business picked up.

He started noticing magazine ads and trade show exhibits for Christmas Décor, a holiday and event decorating franchise. Christmas Décor was started to fill a seasonal void for Quality Lawn Care in Lubbock, Texas. The franchisor promotes Christmas Décor as a good add-on for seasonal businesses. Still, Dennis delayed buying the franchise for two years. "I was an independent business person and didn't want to give that up and spend money to have someone show me how to do it," he says.

In 1998, Dennis took the plunge and bought a Christmas Décor franchise. While he keeps financial records separate for Crede Lawn Service and Christmas Décor, he finds the two businesses complement each other nicely. It enables him to keep his nine employees busy all year, add customers, increase the revenue earned per customer, and improve cash flow throughout the year.

"Christmas Décor gives us buying power for the lights, and it doesn't conflict with the other business," Dennis says. "It's a good fit for us. We start putting up Christmas lights in September right about the time the landscaping slows down. We go back and take the lights down in January. Customers really like that part."

More recently, Dennis bought another franchise, Nite Time Décor, Inc., for landscape and architectural lighting installation and maintenance, from the same franchisor. This, too, is an add-on business that grows Dennis's overall operation. "I bought it to fill a gap and it became part of the core business," he says. "I wanted to make lighting a complete division of the company."

The three businesses provide cross marketing for each other. When Dennis's employees install Christmas lights, they mention that the company also does landscaping and landscape lighting. When they work at landscape clients' homes or businesses, they remind the clients of the other services. Some customers use two or all three services. Others use just one.

Company trucks bear the signs of all three companies. "Come September, when people see our trucks out and about, one neighbor after another calls us," Dennis says. "We have been doing it for so long and taking care of customers that people now recognize our name. We get most of our business word-of-mouth."

While the franchises and the independent landscaping business complement each other as far as the work is concerned, the combination creates more work for Dennis than a single company of the same size. "Even though you buy a franchise and you think you just have to run it as they advise, you still have to work it to fit the economy and area in which you live," Dennis says. "The franchisor will help you, but you still have to make it fit."

MARKETING

■ ■ ■

The franchisor has primary responsibility to build the brand and often charges an advertising fee for promotional activities. But marketing involves many duties that can best be done by the individual franchisee. The most successful franchisees don't rely solely on the franchisor's marketing.

They build relationships in their communities, provide outstanding customer service, and continually communicate with their customers. All of
these activities are key marketing tools and techniques that build individual
as well as systemwide success. Without strong marketing efforts, a franchisee struggles.

74. THE IMPORTANCE OF GOOD MARKETING SKILLS

Franchisees must hone their marketing skills because they are
closest to the customers and best able to learn their needs.

■ ■ ■

One of the highly valued services that comes with most franchise
purchases is marketing and advertising, but the successful franchisee has
or develops strong marketing skills, says Ed Teixeira. In the 1990s, Ed was
both an executive with Staff Builders Home Health Care in Lake Success,
New York, and a multi-million-dollar franchisee with six offices.

"Home health care is not an easy industry to do business in because it
is highly regulated," says Ed, now owner of FranchiseKnowHow LLC in
Stony Brook, New York. Staff Builders spun off its home health care business in 1999. "The key to Staff Builders' marketing was to be able to demonstrate to our referral sources—doctors, hospital discharge personnel, and
insurance companies—that we had the credentials and credibility to take
care of people in their own homes."

Franchisees who lack good marketing skills have a tougher time suc-
ceeding. The franchisee is the best person to get to know the customers or
patients, Ed says. They are on the scene to listen to customers, identify
their need, and find a way to fill that need. "Most of the time, if you execute
the basics of marketing, you'll do fine. The basis of our marketing was that
we provided care that we would expect for ourselves."

Staff Builders could write advertising copy and brochures that said
wonderful things about the company's credentials and level of care, but
each franchisee had to deliver what was promised. "A franchise can have
a package or program for marketing that is cookie-cutter, just as it does for

other operational systems, but what marks the successful franchisees are those who execute the work," Ed says.

Patients and their loved ones who sometimes were the ones arranging for the home health care were the judges of the quality of that care and service. They would give feedback to the people making the referrals, which would be the basis for future work. Testimonials from satisfied patients and requests for Staff Builders the next time care was required were also marketing benefits from the quality service.

In a service franchise, the franchisee sets the tone in his own business but also must rely on employees who love their work, are motivated to provide great care, and receive incentives to serve. The franchisee must establish standards of behavior for employees and then continually train and reinforce that behavior so that employees habitually put their best foot forward with patients, their relatives, and the people who make referrals.

"Many franchisees don't realize that great employees who give great service are part of marketing, but employees' work converts into more customers and more revenue," Ed says. "You need all the marketing tools, but you have to use them to deliver."

In Ed's Staff Builder offices, employees could earn incentives for their efforts. The company had contests for such prizes as televisions to keep employees motivated and feeling good about working for the franchisee. Ed continually looked for ways to show his employees that their work was vital to his business.

75. DO YOUR OWN MARKETING

A franchisee must do local marketing and not depend exclusively on the franchisor's efforts to build a brand.

■ ■ ■

Scott Bailey had many years of success as a salesman for corporations, but when his employer started struggling, he decided he wanted to be in business for himself. "I liked the idea of a franchise because it was a proven success, and I just had to apply it here," Scott says. "But I didn't want to wear a paper hat to work in an all-cash retail business that would chain me to the store 24/7." In 1994 Scott bought a Sandler Sales Institute, a sales and sales management training franchise, in Irvine, California.

He quickly learned that the franchisor's regional advertising and efforts to build the brand were not enough marketing for his individual franchise to succeed. "Sandler is not set up to do all the marketing for you," he says. "Their attitude is 'this is a sales training organization. Go sell.' If I couldn't sell, people wouldn't come to us."

Building a marketing program and a clientele takes time, Scott says. While now he gets most of his business from referrals from previous clients, that wasn't always the case, and he doesn't rely solely on referrals to keep his business growing.

One of his marketing tools is a lunchtime workshop in basic sales techniques. The expectation is that some of the attendees will sign up for more lucrative, in-depth training programs. Initially, Scott offered these workshops for free, but found that many people didn't value the session and didn't even bother to show up. By charging $25, he found people were more committed to attend. He waives the fee if people ask, but they still have a perception that the workshop has value. "There's still the problem of some people who come and pay their money and think their sales problems are fixed," he says, adding that his introductory workshops are just a taste of what clients can learn and achieve with good sales training.

Scott has found that networking is his best marketing tool. He attends local leads groups, business organizations, chambers of commerce, and other events where he can meet face-to-face with other business people to explain the benefits of Sandler sales training. "Even though we get most of our business from referrals, we can't stop networking," he says. "People don't wake up in the morning and say, 'Oh, I need sales training.' We have to educate them to the value." Scott attends all the groups at one time or other, but finds that some groups don't bring in much business and some do initially, but their value diminishes over time. Networking has to be continually assessed for its value to the business. Scott also looks for unusual places to network. "I find at least one golf tournament a month to play in," he says. "That's fun and effective for me."

Scott has found that advertising in the local general circulation newspapers and business publications is not effective for attracting new business, but getting listed in the publications' event calendars and on Web sites of local events is effective.

He also cross-markets within his own program offerings. Scott works with individuals and companies. His corporate division works with big companies that pay a retainer and send employees to Sandler for sales training. He also offers pre-employment assessments of job candidates to identify those with the greatest sales potential. Companies that use the assessments are also candidates for the ongoing corporate sales training programs, and the company leaders are candidates for his "presidents' club."

76. YOU MUST BUILD PERSONAL RELATIONSHIPS

The individual franchisee can best market by developing contacts within the community that bring in more business.

■ ■ ■

Jay Patel's family was in the retail industry in the Caribbean and when he moved to Charlotte, North Carolina, he wanted to own a business. He didn't have the capital to invest in hotels like many of his relatives, so he bought a Mail Boxes Etc. franchise in 1990. In 2001, package shipping giant UPS bought Mail Boxes Etc. and in 2003, the entire franchise system started changing their brand name to The UPS Store name.

Under either name, the franchisor provides a valuable brand, one of the strengths of successful franchises and a key to successful marketing. UPS does advertising of the name change and of the products and services provided by all The UPS Stores.

However, Jay has learned throughout his years of business ownership that the individual franchisee is responsible for marketing his own store. The franchisee can do what a global company cannot: develop personal friendships in the community and with customers. The most effective marketing for small businesses—and make no mistake, most franchisees are small businesses—is relationship building. This type of marketing requires personal time and effort to attend local events, learn customers' names and needs, and proactively seeking ways to meet those needs.

"Like any other business, I need integrated marketing programs through the PTAs and the churches," Jay says. "Consumers have many choices, but if they have a relationship and trust with me, they will do business with me instead of my competitors."

Over the years Jay has sponsored youth sports teams and various expos to get his business name known throughout the community. He has helped charities, such as the "We Deliver Dreams" program to help the underprivileged in Charlotte. He is a member of the city's Hospitality and Tourism Alliance that promotes the area. Such involvement has strengthened ties with people in various businesses and community activities. The more they know Jay, the more likely they are to use his shipping, faxing, copying, and other services. In fact, being involved in his community gives him the opportunity to explain that Mail Boxes Etc. was more than private postal services and The UPS Store is more than shipping.

Most important is building relationships with customers, Jay says. "That's what we do, try to get to know customers personally. If you go to the post office, it's government run, the clerks can't make individual adjustments. We have flexibility to give customers credit and to make their work easier."

Now that Jay is successful, he has been able to invest in hotels and is a regional director for North Carolina of the Asian American Hotel Owners Association, a national trade organization. That involvement also helps Jay build his UPS Store business through relationships he is making in the hospitality industry. For one example, hotel guests often leave possessions behind, and Jay is suggesting to hotel owners that they can ship those items back using The UPS Store. Such an approach can help the hotel owner satisfy his guests and bring more business to The UPS Store.

77. CUSTOMER SERVICE IS THE FRANCHISEE'S IMPERATIVE

One of the strengths of franchising is having ownership on the front lines with customers to make sure they receive the service that brings them back.

■ ■ ■

In 1993, Wayne and Dee Hendricks were running separate companies for other owners. They decided they could combine their experience and talent and build their own business together. They decided to go the franchise route to get support in an unfamiliar industry and national buying power. As they researched various franchises, PostNet Postal and Business Services kept coming up. "We were impressed with this company because it was family-owned and strong on service to its franchisees," says Wayne, who owns the PostNet in Glendale, Arizona.

As the company name states, this is a service business, providing pack and ship services, copies, Internet time, resumes, digital printing, fax services, and more. Each PostNet doesn't survive on sales of packaging supplies and passport photos and rental of private mailboxes. It survives and grows on service. The franchisor certainly sets the tone and expectation for the level of service and can model it by the level of service it provides to franchisees. But each owner must multiply and deliver that service to the customers in order to succeed, Wayne says.

"Once we decided which franchise to buy, we made a total commitment and left our other jobs to devote full time to the business," he says. "It's a good brand and competitive prices, but customer service is incredible. That's what sets us apart from the other postal and business service companies."

When a potential customer first comes to Wayne, he spends time understanding what the customer needs before trying to sell anything. This approach requires a personality comfortable with planting seeds for future customer relationships, Wayne says. His definition of customer service includes prompt, professional results and the highest level of workmanship.

The franchisor helps educate, train, and improve customer service throughout the system with periodic meetings throughout the year. "They have brought in programs to reinstill the importance of customer service, but the franchisees also have to have the personality for it," Wayne says.

His background was in manufacturing and Dee's was in construction. Even in those very different industries, both valued customer service as means of attracting and keeping customers. Customer service is valuable in every industry as a means of differentiating one brand above another. Studies have indicated that customers like to be loyal to a company, but only if they get the service they expect.

The franchisor can offer all the training it wants, but the franchisee must show up for the events. "I never miss a convention or the opportunity to learn new stuff that PostNet comes out with," Wayne says. "I don't need as much help as I used to but still I learn something new every day. I could be very committed to the industry but not do that on my own because we franchisees are busy running our businesses every day."

After exposure to customer service training, the franchisee must be willing to build it into the individual store. Wayne did that so well that PostNet named the Hendrickses franchisees of the year in 2004. "That's something we can share with our customers to illustrate that we are serious about what we're doing for them," Wayne says.

78. CONSTANT FOLLOW-UP AND REMINDERS

The successful franchisee has the habit of staying in touch with
past customers and current prospects.

■ ■ ■

There's no secret to Louise and Gary Heidenreich's success as Neshanic Station, New Jersey, franchisees of Jet-Black International, which repairs and seals asphalt driveways. They treat the name of every lead, contact, and customer as golden. "When we bought the franchise (in 2002), we were not fully aware of all the back-end work," Louise says. "Customer interface is vital. We have to call, answer their questions, several times. Even after we schedule a job, I follow up with a phone call to make sure they know what we are doing or if we are delayed. If anyone calls with an issue, we will go back and fix it. We let them know we do that."

Traditionally, part-timers and itinerant workers have dominated the asphalt and seal-coating industry. The franchise brings permanency and quality control. These factors open the possibility for repeat and referral business for the franchisee who maintains contact with customers.

Driveway repair is a seasonal business, primarily April through October. The Heidenreiches approach business as a team in order to maximize their efficiency in the shortened work season. Gary handles sales, and Louise does the office work, job scheduling, and follow-up. "When we hit the season, we live, breathe, and eat this business," Louise says.

The franchisor helps generate leads by sending out postcards to a franchisee's customer base in the early part of the year. Gary follows up with quotes during April and May. Then Louise follows up those contacts by sending reminder postcards to the most promising jobs. Seal coating lasts about three years, so the Heidenreiches keep contact information on past customers to remind them when it is time to reseal.

Perhaps it's not surprising that the Heidenreiches are familiar with customer follow-up. They have owned several high-end retail businesses, including fitness equipment and hot tubs. Cultivating customers is a necessity in retailing, especially when the products have a high price tag.

"In Jet-Black, we can be twice as expensive as some competitors," Louise says. "We are blessed to be in an affluent area, so many people value quality. But when customers ask why we charge so much, we go through every reason with them, and the last thing we tell them is 'you get us.' We don't mean it as a joke. We provide the best service and follow-up."

When the Heidenreiches were looking for a business to buy in 2000, they decided they no longer wanted to be in retailing, which has long hours and requires a constant presence in the store. While Jet-Black requires a great deal of customer contact, the franchise can be run from home, and the equipment and supplies can be kept in an out-of-the-way, low-cost warehouse. They don't have to pay for a location with high exposure. "We knew nothing about seal coating, but we saw quality as we were used to in our retail businesses, a system, and people with a lot of integrity to help us," Louise says. "We have employees to apply the seal coating, but not to do customer follow-up. They don't take the time to treat each one with care. To us (as owners) a name, a lead, a customer is someone we can do something for."

79. MARKETING THROUGH COMMUNITY INVOLVEMENT

When a franchisee is new in town just showing up frequently and persistently can be the best way to build brand recognition.

■ ■ ■

Patrice Mudd grew up on a farm in Wyoming where her family raised their own food. She developed a discerning taste for fresh, top-quality food. She also developed an appreciation for a sense of community that pervades smaller towns. After running a pet supply store for 14 years in Lake Forest, California, Patrice thought her town wanted but did not have that sense of community.

"I wanted to start an ice cream store," Patrice says. "Ice cream parlors give kids a safe place to go and (a place) for parents to take the family on outings."

In 2003, she and husband Joe signed a franchise agreement for five Maggie Moo's Ice Cream and Treatery stores. "We did a lot of research of all the ice cream franchises and Maggie Moo's had the best ice cream," says Patrice, who went around the country personally tasting various cool offerings and relying on her farm-honed taste buds. Obviously, the Mudds weren't alone. Many dessert franchises are elbowing for good locations in suburban markets across the country. The Mudds recognized that they needed to do something to generate awareness of their ice cream shops and to create a following of local customers so in love with Maggie Moo's ice cream that they would drive past competitors' locations to eat at Maggie Moo's.

Drawing on her experiences with close-knit communities, Patrice has become active in neighborhood schools, churches, and charitable events. They offer free ice cream for local events, to introduce the Maggie Moo's name and incomparable ice cream taste to area residents. The Mudds don't scrimp on the ice cream they donate. It is the same premium ice cream made in the stores. Anything of lesser quality would defeat the purpose of this community involvement, Patrice says. The goal is to fix in people's minds the wonderful taste that they can't get anywhere other than Maggie Moo's. "They can sample our ice cream in the store too, as much as they want," she says. "All the time I hear, 'Wow! I can't believe the taste.' Once they're hooked on the taste, they don't just buy a cone, they might buy a pint to eat in front of the fire at home or (an ice cream) cake for a party."

Getting the word and taste out into the community requires persistence, Patrice says. "You have to get your name out there. It's like looking for a boyfriend. You're not going to get one unless you're out and about giving hugs and smiles." Yet each target neighborhood is a little different, she adds. "We started four stores at one time, and each store's neighborhood has its personality. Balboa Island is a tourist destination. Ladera Ranch is a planned community. Lake Forest and Laguna Niguel yearn to bring people together in community."

Because giving ice cream samples away is expensive, a franchisee must use common sense and not say yes to every request, Patrice says. The goal is to reach as many ice cream buyers as possible. Schools are good venues because kids love ice cream and tell their parents. Business events can be productive because local business owners like to support other small-business owners and appreciate when a fellow entrepreneur is being a good citizen in the community.

"Like a good relationship, it takes time to build your name in the community," Patrice says. "You're not going to see immediate (increases in sales). It takes a lot of time and persistence."

80. A PROVEN TRACK RECORD FOR QUALITY

A franchise system can collect information and experiences over a large area to reinforce marketing claims of success and proven performance.

■ ■ ■

Chuck Heaps retired after 21 years in the Air Force and wanted a second career that would allow him to live near Beale Air Force Base in the Sierra Mountains of California. He discovered ServiceMaster Clean, which offered several different franchises including disaster restoration services, and remembered an experience his parents had years before. While they were spending the winter in Arizona, pipes burst in their Iowa home destroying the carpeting. "I could personally appreciate the importance of having a qualified and reliable support system to help put things back together again," Chuck says. "I looked at the fact that ServiceMaster had been franchising since the '50s and had a reputation for quality service and uncompromised standards."

Chuck opened ServiceMaster of the Foothills in 1988, to specialize in correcting water and fire damage to homes and commercial buildings.

With thousands of franchisees and decades of recordkeeping, Service-Master can prove the value of its services, Chuck says. That has been an invaluable marketing tool with insurance companies, insurance agents, and other referral sources for work. "It used to be that a homeowner with flooding or fire damage had to get three estimates and the insurance company would wait to pick the lowest price," Chuck says. "ServiceMaster nationwide has sold all the major insurance companies that if we can get in within 24 hours, we have a 75 percent chance of saving the carpet or wood floors. After the next 24 hours we have a 35 percent chance and it goes down from there."

That type of performance over a long period of time in many different markets has brought many jobs to franchisees without a long bidding process, he says. To qualify, the franchisees must have around-the-clock phone answering and the ability to send workers out within two to four hours. They must have the specialized equipment to do the job correctly and training to assess the needed repairs, such as the skill to determine the amount of humidity within a structure.

"We allow the insurance companies to tap into our computers to see their losses by region, by cause of the damage," he says. "They can't do that on their own computers. We track and offer validated value nationwide so we can show how much money we save them by fast response."

All franchisees contribute to the national advertising fund. Chuck also has his own marketing person talking with individual insurance agents, plumbers, and other referral partners. He and 30 other ServiceMaster franchisees in his region pool their resources to market to insurance companies' regional offices. "Insurance offices are centralized and our marketers kept running into each other," Chuck says. "The insurance guys said 'You're good, but we don't need to see three of you to tell us.'"

There is a plus to having thousands of disaster restoration franchisees driving home their track record for quality. ServiceMaster can pool the resources of several franchisees to tackle big jobs that no independent company or single franchisee could do alone, Chuck says. After terrorists flew an airplane into the Pentagon on September 11, 2001, ServiceMaster brought together representatives from 51 franchises for disaster restoration. The call went out within a couple of hours of the attack, and ServiceMaster technicians were on the job the same day, working around the clock while Pentagon employees continued their work. "I don't think one business could handle that size of loss if it weren't a franchise," Chuck says.

81. THE NEED FOR MARKETING OUTSIDE OF YOUR TERRITORY

Franchisees can work together to market their individual
businesses while honoring exclusive territorial rights.

■ ■ ■

Susan Phelan worked in the software industry for 23 years, but
wanted to break away from the high technology industry, so she worked
with a life coach to define a new direction for her career. In 2004, she discovered and bought a Home Instead Senior Care franchise in Chicago, Illinois. The company provides nonmedical care and companionship for the
elderly. The right to serve a particular elderly client goes to the franchisee
who owns the territory in which the client lives. Even so, Susan has discovered the need and benefit of marketing outside her own territory.

Many franchisors grant exclusive territories for providing services or
selling products, and most franchisees want such exclusivity. The arrangement prevents franchisees from taking business from colleagues who sup-
posedly are on the same team. However, the issue of marketing beyond
territorial boundaries is less certain. Often, franchisees don't consider this
approach. The franchisor does the regional and national advertising to build
the brand name, which benefits everyone in the system. Franchisees are allowed and expected to market locally, which often involves such activities
as networking and building referrals that complement paid advertising.

In fact, it might seem that marketing outside one's own territory would
be a waste of money and effort for the individual franchisee, but not in certain types of services. Home Instead Senior Care gets its business from
three sources: the elderly person in need of assistance, family members of
the elderly person, and referral entities that range from hospitals to members of the clergy.

"The definition of territory needs to be black and white about which
franchisee gets to service a client," Susan says. "But in reality, the sphere
of influence for that client might be much wider. The son or daughter might
live (outside the exclusive territory), or the client might live in one territory
but be in the hospital in another territory."

Susan's territory has few hospitals where she would normally market Home Instead services. So she has worked out an arrangement with a neighboring franchisee to jointly market in the hospitals in his territory.

"The nature of my territory has brought out the marketing skills I developed in the software industry," she says. "Some marketers would only approach one person per hospital. I'm a more thorough marketer. I go to the whole hospital and build lots and lots of contacts within one hospital."

Her marketing work is a winning formula for both franchisees. They both get more referrals from the hospital, depending on where individual patients live. Susan has learned that pitching to fellow franchisees her extraterritorial marketing request as a benefit rather than an intrusion tends to make them more agreeable to the idea.

"It is absolutely a no-lose situation," Susan says. "Sometimes business owners get this attitude that 'you're in my sandbox' instead of saying, 'This is a gift. Thank you very much.' I'm helping my neighboring franchise, I know it."

Marketing for referrals, while one of the strongest tools for individual franchisees, takes time to pay off, Susan says. "People need to see and hear your name multiple times. But eventually enough buzz has been created that the phone starts to ring. Even after developing your referral network it makes sense to continue marketing outside your own territory because relationships require constant contact and reminders."

82. THE VALUE OF SPECIALIZATION

A franchisee who could serve multiple markets may be more successful emphasizing one niche, especially when starting out.

■ ■ ■

David Mains was a paralegal working for law practices in Niceville, Florida, and wife, Joanie, spent 20 years in the Air Force. But they had long wanted to own a business of their own. After Joanie retired from the military, the Mains answered dozens of newspaper advertisements for business opportunities and businesses for sale. One was for ColorGlo International, which specialized in products and services to restore and repair fabric. After watching demonstrations of redying carpets, the Mains knew they could run this business and opened ColorGlo International for the Emerald Coast in Niceville in 1994.

Initially, it seemed to be an advantage that anyone with faded or damaged fabric was a potential customer, David says. The proprietary products can be used on car seats, door panels, carpet and vinyl roofs, dining room chairs, boat beds, airplane seats, and pool liners. Other products can deodorize nursing homes and remove mildew. Still others repair cracks and cigarette burns. "When we started out, we did everything," David says. "After we learned to use the products, it was a matter of doing the work."

But trying to service too many diverse markets can put a strain on the marketing efforts of a small business. Although the franchisor provides broad-based marketing and advertising to build name recognition, each franchisee must build a personal customer base. Relationships, referrals, and quality work are common tools for the franchisee. If the franchisee seeks broad residential, commercial, marine, and aviation markets, all his time can easily be spent on marketing. The franchisee needs employees to do the work. Many franchisees, like the Mains, decide they want to do the work themselves and keep their business small. In that case, the franchisee's marketing tends to move the business into a niche. For the Mains, that niche is automotive.

"We cultivated auto dealerships in our area," David says. "We have three main dealers. When they buy cars or take them in trade, we clean and repair all the fabric. It is repeat business. We haven't advertised in years, and we still get calls from people saying, 'everyone says you do a great job.' We also get referrals from the car dealers."

One reason David started focusing on one niche was the competition from similar types of companies. Instead of educating new customers about ColorGlo's capabilities, David got plenty of business from satisfied customers and the people they referred. He gets calls from people who used his services years before and now have another need. This type of marketing is easier and more efficient. "Once you find a niche, you have much less competition," David says.

The Mains also have a few secondary niches they will serve, such as custom dying of clothing, for example, dying shoes to match an outfit. But there are other industries David avoids. "I just turned down a 40-foot boat. I would rather focus on the auto dealerships. We can be selective (about) who we work for. By specializing, we can be the best."

83. THE COST OF ACQUIRING CUSTOMERS

A franchisee must be mindful of the most efficient methods of marketing in order to be as profitable as possible while building the business.

After working as a certified public accountant and in corporate finance, Kirk Mathers came to a point in his career that he believed he had enough experience either to start his own company or to buy a franchise. He happened to explore franchising first. He looked at a maid service and educational assistance before buying a franchise for The Alternative Board, small-group executive groups, in Gilbert, Arizona, in 2004, naming his business Next Level Advisory Team LLC. "They needed my skills as a chief financial officer and CPA. I could provide immediate help," he explains. "I also bought a franchise because I wanted a proven business model. Part of the system is marketing. They have all the marketing materials ready to go."

Like most franchisors, The Alternative Board offers a variety of marketing tools and programs, such as Web sites for franchisee facilitators, and regional and co-op advertising. But Kirk, leaning on his finance background, says each franchisee needs to evaluate his marketing efforts and choose the most cost effective methods. "A critical success factor is customer acquisition at the least possible cost," he says.

Direct mail is a method advocated by the franchisor, which will identify 2,000 prospects within a franchisee's territory who match the demographics of executives likely to join one of the small discussion groups. A franchisee can pay to send out direct mail solicitations two or six times a year, Kirk says. He can also comb through the mailing list for his area and cull companies that seem less likely to sign up, for example if the revenues are too low or that particular industry is struggling in Arizona. Then he can send direct mail to a core list of 1,000 or 2,000 names. Kirk can pay for telemarketing calls to follow up on the mailings or for phone calls instead of direct mail.

Kirk has created his own database of likely prospects for direct mail marketing and for e-mails as well, using ACT! contact management software. He also created his own electronic newsletter. "These are 250 names of current prospects whose permission I have to put on my list," he says. "These are people I meet at chamber of commerce mixers, people I know, people I used to work with plus prospects I met the previous month who weren't ready to sign up yet. I mail to them and then follow up in six months. I want to stay in touch because it takes some executives a long time to decide that The Alternative Board is right for them."

He could also sit in the office and make cold calls. "Is it worth $600 a month in my time and only being able to touch half as many people? I haven't done it," he says.

The personal e-mail list is the least expensive, the easiest for regular contact, and often the most productive, he says.

"New franchisees don't realize how long it takes to recruit business owners," Kirk says. "You do your financial projections for 24 months, cut your anticipated revenue in half, and double your time for building a customer base. Then decide if you can live with that worst-case scenario."

That simple financial exercise helps franchisees realize the importance of finding the least costly, most effective marketing methods and then sticking with them, he says, adding, "Business start-ups take more time than you imagine."

GROWTH

■ ■ ■

Many franchisees are ambitious to grow beyond a single location. The franchisor should welcome that effort. Many encourage and assist it, but the franchisee shouldn't sit back and wait for guidance from the franchisor. Technology that helps the franchisee analyze the business is helpful to the one-unit operator, but it's essential for the growth-oriented franchisee. Even the best systems have room for improvement. Many of the best ideas come from franchisees who are dealing with operations and customers daily. Those ideas can help grow the individual franchise and, if the franchisor is wise, the system.

84. TECHNOLOGY DRIVES SUCCESS

A franchisee can correct problems quickly by measuring and
continually monitoring business performance.

■ ■ ■

While running 50 Church's Chicken restaurants in Los Angeles, California, Aslam Khan used his Lotus 1-2-3 spreadsheet software to analyze the performance of each unit. "It was my hobby. I wanted to know what happens in business and why," he explains. The practice turned the units from money losers into the best in the chain.

Aslam brought his spreadsheets and analytical ways with him when he formed Falcon Holdings LLC in Oakbrook, Illinois, to buy Atlanta Franchise Development Co., a money-losing Church's Chicken franchisee with restaurants in the Midwest in 1999. The company had an information technology department, and one worker said he could automate Aslam's system for instantaneous data updates.

"What usually happens in a company is the profit and loss statement comes in five weeks after the fact and it takes the executives a week to go through it and know they have a problem," Aslam says. "We get real-time information. Go into our conference room and you can see the computer screen with the numbers changing as it goes. Our field people can go online to find out the numbers, but we don't wait. Our IT people push that information out to the stores."

That information is not just gross sales. Aslam analyzes dozens of measures: discounts, voids, overages, taxes, white meat versus dark meat consumption, and cost of goods sold down to the single napkin.

When Aslam first acquired Atlanta Franchise Development Co., the franchisee was $5 million in the red. It is now profitable thanks to the strict, technology-driven financial monitoring system, and is the largest Church's Chicken franchisee with 101 restaurants in Illinois, Indiana, Michigan, Missouri, Ohio, and Virginia. One thing he had to change was store managers' mindset. Following his motto of "inform, influence, and engage," Aslam gave them the financial performance data and rewarded them for improvement. By 6:00 AM each morning, a manager knows the store's performance from the previous day and the numbers that need to be improved by noon. Stores are ranked by their performance each day and managers can compare each measure to that of every other store. In 2004, Aslam gave each store manager a laptop computer to encourage even greater attention to the financial numbers. "We're turning our people into knowledgeable businesspeople, not just store managers," Aslam says.

When the financial system was first instituted, restaurants' actual food costs were 3 percent to 4 percent higher than the established ideal. Within five years it was less than 2 percent.

"Cost of goods sold, that's what makes or breaks you. Then labor," Aslam says. "Our cost of food is 30-some percent. For the parent company, it's 33 percent. That 3 percent (difference) is $61 million a year."

That's why the franchisor asked Aslam to implement his real-time financial monitoring system throughout the chain.

But Aslam isn't just a bean counter. He had been manager of the American Club at the U.S. embassy in his native Pakistan. When he first came to the United States, a Church's Chicken franchise in Los Angeles wouldn't hire him as manager, so he started as a team member. He still visits his restaurants every week and monitors the grease buildup on the counters. "I like neat and clean restaurants," he says. "But I also want to make a lot of money for all my employees."

85. CONTRIBUTE TO IMPROVING THE SYSTEM

Franchisors that encourage franchisees to improve the system
are most likely to thrive.

■ ■ ■

Don Duncan and Bill Buczek first became involved with Valpak Direct Marketing Systems Inc. 12 years before the company started selling franchises. The Largo, Florida, cooperative direct mail firm started selling distributorships in the early 1970s, and Don and Bill were among the first 15 distributors when they bought the rights to sell coupon ads in Detroit, Michigan, in 1976. They became a franchisee when the company started selling franchises in 1988.

"I had been a salesperson in the pharmaceutical industry, and one of the things that appealed to me was that this was sales oriented," Don says. "All the (Valpak) founder wanted to do was printing; the dealers were the sales force. I know what a printing press is, but I don't know how to turn it on. I don't know how to stuff envelopes.

"You should ask yourself, if you're going to be happy doing the day-to-day work of what the franchise does," he adds. "If we didn't expand, I was happy doing the basic work."

But Don and Bill's franchise did expand, adding the Denver territory to the company. Now they are the largest Valpak franchisee with 69 employees between the two locations.

However, in the early years, few customers knew the Valpak name or even what cooperative direct mail was. That gave Don and Bill the freedom and responsibility to build and improve the Valpak system. Initially, co-op direct mailers would not put coupons from competing companies in the same mailing. Don and Bill were the first to change that, a method called open marketing. In the old days, cooperative mailings went out every other month or quarterly. Don and Bill were the first to initiate monthly mailings.

"The industry was moving in that direction but no one had done it yet," Don says. "Now everyone does it. The mindset of older dealers was that if they mailed six times a year they could take a lot of vacations. There wasn't a lot of competition in the early days, but as competition increased, it became more like a business with tighter profit margins. The franchisor supported what we were doing. They gave us financial support because our concepts made everyone more money, so of course the franchisor was very interested in that."

Don bought the Denver market from another franchisee and the move gave a career growth opportunity to one of Don's good employees. That operation also gave the franchisee some separate but related business opportunities such as a coupon magazine. "As long as we maintain our production with Valpak, the franchisor doesn't object to us doing some other things," Don says.

Such expansions are not a good idea if a franchisee is struggling, he adds. "If they're not doing well, some people grasp at straws and add unrelated things. It's important to do one thing and do it right."

Valpak has grown to a franchise network that mails tens of billions of coupons each year. Both the franchisor and franchisees have improved the sophistication of the operation, including proprietary business management software that makes back-office functions seamless for the franchisees, Don says. Franchisees can take national or multimarket orders and share revenues with each other. "Everything is much more coordinated than in the old days," he says.

86.   DON'T WAIT FOR THE FRANCHISOR

In most franchise systems, the franchisee has freedom and
sometimes encouragement to make improvements in the
individual business.

■ ■ ■

Dorene Pennell and her father John Bledsoe bought a PIP Printing
and Document Services franchise in South Hadley, Massachusetts, in
1985. Eighteen months later Dorene's husband Wendell came on board to
operate the printing press and run his separate trucking broker service from
a back office. Eventually he joined PIP full time to handle sales and marketing. Dorene oversees production, and John does the accounting.

The printing industry has been changing and diminishing for years.
The Pennells had three locations at one time, but now have one location
doing more business than ever. The secret to surviving in a shrinking industry is to dare to try something new, Wendell says. "As the industry
changes you have to adapt or die. If you're doing the same things you did
15 years ago, you won't make it. We're no longer just printing; we're a
communications company, a full-service business partner for our clients."

The South Hadley franchise was the first to add mailing services, for
example. While other PIP locations were not growing, Wendell became an
expert in postal regulations to offer the services to his clients. Now putting
address labels on clients' mailings accounts for 20 percent of the franchisee's sales. He started giving seminars to other PIP franchisees and handled the mailing services for all the PIPs in New England, which paid for
special equipment to fold, insert, address, and meter large volumes of mail.
As those franchisees sell more mailing services, they buy their own equipment to do their work in-house.

The Pennells are not content to sit back and wait for the franchisor to
impose ideas or systems. They jump on new ideas as soon as they hear
them. PIP does not prohibit its franchisees from adding additional profit
centers, Wendell says. "The franchisor does require a certain mix of services, but I could sell hot dogs as long as I pay royalties on them." The

franchisor has gotten better at seeing industry trends in recent years, but Wendell isn't waiting to be told how to build his business.

When the Pennells started hearing about variable data printing in the late 1990s, they quickly added the service in their store. Wendell describes it as "mail merge on steroids." A mail piece not only inserts the name of the recipient in the salutation, it inserts personalized information and photos throughout the copy. The Pennells provide variable data mailing programs for car dealers that have extensive databases on their customers. A buyer might receive a letter from the dealer that includes a photo of the car he bought, the name of the salesman, and pertinent facts about himself. The franchisor has adopted variable data mailing programs systemwide, based on what the Pennells did.

"We have become a marketing machine because we do it for others. We learn from our clients and then apply that idea to our business. We use variable data on our own prospects list and for a little money have a top-quality mailing. We get more phone calls not just because they're curious but because they want to do projects," Wendell says. He turns around and shares those successes with other PIP franchisees. "Another franchisee has the same mail equipment I have. I do $20,000 a month in work using that equipment and he does $2,000, so I spent half an hour on the phone telling him how to improve his sales. In franchising, you depend on each other. You're not just a lone wolf."

87. BUILD ANOTHER LEVEL OF OPPORTUNITY

Service franchisees may be able to multiply their opportunities
by developing ways to use their services to grow their
franchisor's system.

■ ■ ■

Eric Dombach was a corporate trainer who was tired of traveling so much and being an employee. He started developing a business model to open his own consulting and coaching practice. Then he searched the Internet looking for a way to get a faster jump on business ownership. He found Action International Business Coaching and decided in 2001 to buy a franchise in Lancaster, Pennsylvania, rather than spend years developing the systems and resources that Action offered.

Some business coaches are refugees from the corporate wars, seeking to work part time, but not Eric. Within two years, he was Action's U.S. business coach of the year and within three years he was global coach of the year. His franchise grew 140 percent a year. He brought in coaching associates to build his franchise to $1 million in annual revenues within three years. He coached other coaches within Action and was a "gold coach," the designation for the very best people in the global franchise network. But that level of success is not enough for Eric.

Eric created two related businesses to provide the technical writing that helps clients develop the infrastructure needed to grow their companies to the next level and to do telemarketing for coaches' seminars that are part of the Action system. Still, even that is not enough for Eric.

"There is a developing franchisee-to-franchisee economy in which we sell (products and services) to each other," Eric explains. "It's a very healthy thing. Action has a coaches' coach. I did that for a while in Pennsylvania. Then I was a global coach trainer. Now I have created what we call 'the firm coach' that accepts only gold coaches and helps them grow."

The concept is to take the best coaches, who are grossing $100,000 to $200,000 a year and grow them to the multi-million-dollar level in exchange for a percentage of the increased revenue for life. Some of those receiving this assistance will become certified as firm coaches to help others grow. "You can't attract coaches to do this unless the financial reward is substantial," Eric explains.

Rather than discourage or block Eric's idea, the franchisor actually suggested it. Eric said he was tired of coaching individual clients and wondered what else he could do. Action executives suggested that he find the best Action coaches and help them grow. The idea didn't even have a name initially and Eric is creating the structure as he goes.

"Action has a basic legal structure that governs, but within that boundary there is a lot of freedom," Eric says. "As long as I grow the franchises, it's good for all of us."

Eric loves franchising and wants to remain a franchisee as he builds this new level of coaching for other Action franchisees. "The upside of franchising has been so massive for me," he says. "A lot of people say, 'don't you resent it?' I say, 'why?' I started with $9,000 and I was a millionaire three-and-a-half years later."

88. GROWTH BY ADDING TERRITORIES

The most successful franchisees own more than one unit,
sometimes becoming virtual minifranchisors by purchasing
territorial development rights.

■ ■ ■

When Sunil Rupani bought a Wireless Toyz franchise in Brownsville, Texas, in 2003, he and his family already owned an independent jewelry store and a franchise in a different industry. His ambition was to own multiple businesses to build greater revenues than a single business could on its own.

But Sunil felt immediate affinity with Wireless Toyz corporate officers and the existing franchisees. "The corporate officers were humble, and I immediately felt a part of the company. I developed a great relationship with CEO Joe Barbat," Sunil says. "Every franchisee went out of his way to help. It wasn't that way at the other franchise I owned."

Wireless Toyz sells multiple brands of wireless products and services, and satellite services. It sounded easy enough that Sunil even explored whether to start an independent competitor. But the franchisor offered pre-negotiated contracts with the major carriers that provided higher payouts than Sunil could get on his own, lower-priced products, and a system of support. So Sunil bought the Brownsville territory, the first Wireless Toyz in Texas. Even though it is a small town, Sunil, who has a marketing background, quickly built his franchise to the fourth highest revenues in the system. That's when he looked around for other opportunities for growth. But instead of looking at other types of franchises and independent businesses to add to his stable, Sunil bought the Wireless Toyz master territories for Brownsville/San Antonio and Houston.

Wireless Toyz wants its individual franchises to be owner operated, but as it expands, the franchisor is seeking middle-level operators to maintain a high level of support for local franchisees while they grow the company.

"I'm at a different level, a developer as well as a franchisee," Sunil says. "I have charge over what happens in my territory, who can come in and who can't, and how much protection to give the franchisee. I'm a buffer for everyone. If a franchisee feels too intimidated to talk to corporate, they can talk to me. I'm going through the same headaches and heartaches they are. If there's a problem, I try to solve it."

These territorial developers, especially common internationally, can build substantial companies while following the franchisor's system. The franchisor usually sets goals for numbers of units to open and deadlines for completion. In Sunil's case, he has ten years to open 30 to 35 stores in the Brownsville/San Antonio territory and 40 to 50 units in Houston. "Corporate was fair about it. They weren't greedy," he says. "My goals are higher than theirs. I want to have close to 100 stores."

His growth approach to selling franchises in his territories has been to approach family members and friends. Not only are they most likely to trust his assurances that their Wireless Toyz franchises will succeed, they are people he trusts most to do the hard work involved in running and growing a franchise. "They can vouch for me best," he adds. "Why would I get my brother involved if I weren't successful? Two of my employees also want stores. They see the success and want in on it. I lose my managers, but I gain franchisees I trust. But I insist that they have their own money invested too. They won't care that it does well unless their own money is at risk."

89. THE MASTER FRANCHISEE

Some buyers obtain rights to a multiple location deal from the
beginning rather than grow a single unit at a time.

■ ■ ■

Grant Fawcett's family had owned six McDonald's restaurant franchises in New Jersey, and he managed them for five years. He later managed corporate executive suites in 12 office buildings in Southern California. Clients could rent the executive suite's meeting rooms and order catered meals for business meetings. The two experiences came together when a franchise broker suggested Grant would be ideal for an Apple Spice Junction franchise, which provides box lunch delivery and catering for business events. It doesn't have walk-in, retail customers; it caters to corporations. "A Domino's delivery system with board food instead of pizza," Grant says.

He could have purchased a single location to deliver just box lunches or he could have owned a single location with both box lunches and catering. Each territory contains approximately 5,000 white collar businesses. He didn't jump into the franchise quickly, spending more than a year investigating and talking with other franchisees. Grant and wife, Amy, who had also worked with him at McDonald's, decided to tighten their belts and pay for a master franchise for two counties in Southern California that can handle 12 to 27 locations. While the up-front investment is substantially more, the royalties are half the standard 6 percent for the system. "The master franchise part was the deciding factor," Grant says. He opened the pilot store in Irvine, California, in 2005 and can now either build additional stores himself or sell franchises to others.

While McDonald's is the best known name in franchising, its system is mature so there is less opportunity for growth and for an experienced business man to have an influence, Grant says. Apple Spice Junction first opened in Utah in 1988, but didn't start franchising until 2002. The downside was that the brand was not yet well known; the upside was that the region was not saturated with too many locations competing not only with other companies but with other Apple Spice Junctions.

"They're still improving, which I see as a plus," he says. "While they offer a turnkey system, I could shop around for better prices. I found a better rate for equipment so (the franchisor) talked to that company about providing equipment nationwide. We franchisees have phone conferences, and I said, 'let's pool our resources and form committees to find cheaper prices and better quality.' The next day, the two gentlemen (Randy Clegg and Wayne Curtis) who run Apple Spice Junction said, 'let's do it.'"

A franchise system has resources that an independent business doesn't. Grant can tap the long experience of the franchisor as well as the management experiences of other Apple Spice Junction franchisees, some of whom come from the restaurant industry and others who have legal, courier, or other business experience that have applications to a delivery business. "I don't mind paying a franchise fee for that access," Grant says.

Grant continued his real estate management job to keep family income steady, and Amy ran the store. "I'm comfortable dealing with (top executives). I have many contacts who I can use to grow Apple Spice Junction," he says. "In my management job I saw a need for this type of service. We don't compete with traditional restaurants, whose food doesn't hold well for

gs. Good food is part of the need, but what's most im-
usiness lunches is that the food shows up and on time."

OVERCOMING TROUBLE

■ ■ ■

Franchising has not been without its difficulties and challenges. Any contractual relationship has disputes that sometimes go all the way to court. The disagreements tear a system apart and drive away business if not handled properly. Seemingly irreparable disputes can be resolved if both sides are willing to work out solutions that are considerate of everyone. No one gets everything he wants, but perhaps a system emerges stronger from the effort. Still, franchising is not for everyone.

90. THE FRANCHISEE MUST AGREE WITH THE BUSINESS MODEL

A franchisor's business model is the framework for the entire
system. A franchisee who does not buy into the approach for
doing business will be unhappy.

■ ■ ■

After working 25 years as a computer programmer and manager for a Japanese-owned information technology company, Gary Gould lost his job when the company downsized. At the same time, his son Erik was looking for a job. So the pair decided to pool their talents in business. "Coming out of the corporate world I had no clue how to run a business," Gary says. "I wanted a proven business model, so I started looking at franchising."

He devoted a great deal of time to talking with many different franchisees in many different systems. "There was a recurring theme. Those who were dissatisfied with their business or franchisor or franchising in general were people who didn't like the way things were done," Gary says. He realized that his own success would depend on finding a franchisor with a proven track record and business model that he and Erik could believe in wholeheartedly. If the approach, operations, corporate culture, and philosophy didn't make sense to Gary, he wouldn't execute it well, and he would end up like those dissatisfied franchisees he had interviewed who didn't like the way things were done.

As he investigated different franchising systems, he quickly eliminated those that would only give him a select list of franchisees to visit and talk with. He wanted to know the franchisor wasn't afraid of what any franchisee in any location might say. "My whole approach was to lessen as much as possible any exposure to all of the many things that can doom a new venture to early failure," he says.

In 2002, Gary and Erik bought a FASTFRAME USA, Inc. franchise in Glen Rock, New Jersey. The custom framing shop started in Newcastle, England, in 1983, opened its first American shop in Thousand Oaks, California, in 1986, and started franchising a year later. The 16-year track record convinced Gary that FASTFRAME had proven its business model and would provide the training and ongoing support he wanted. For example, FASTFRAME has marketing support programs and business development tools including a "Recipe Book" of promotions that have worked for other franchisees. "They provided help with location, pricing, and how to sell. Those are not natural for me, but they are part of the job now," Gary says. "Once you get going, you can do what you want, and they are there if you need help."

FASTFRAME's model requires each store to maintain a huge selection of custom framing materials and molding, provide skilled framing craftsmanship, meet customers' instant deadlines when necessary, and serve both residential and business clients. Corporations sometimes place large orders that franchisees must be able to handle. "We're not a gift shop. If we preframe artwork (for store displays) we do them to show our capabilities, not to be an art museum," Gary says. "I like the business, but it's a lot of work. Don't let anyone tell you a franchise isn't hard work. It's crazy around the holidays."

91. FROM LAWSUITS TO TEAMWORK

Even sour franchise relations can be healed if the franchisor
and franchisees are willing to work and negotiate in good faith.

■ ■ ■

In the early 1990s, North Carolina–based Meineke Car Care Centers
was one of the most publicized battles between a franchisor and its franchisees. A class-action lawsuit filed in 1996 by ten franchisees claimed
that Meineke misused the advertising fund. The franchisees won the largest judgment in franchise history, which was later overturned by a federal
appeals court.

The acrimony predated the lawsuit, says Mark Zuckerman, owner of
nine Meineke shops in New York and Connecticut and one of the founders
of the Meineke Franchisee Association in 1991.

"The franchisor had an aggressive style, very disrespectful of franchisees," says Mark, who has been with the system from its founding, through
this acrimonious period, and to post-lawsuit leadership that has changed its
tone and practices.

"The franchise contract I originally signed (in 1978) was a two-page
document. Now it has become a book," he says. "If you shake hands and
say you're going to do something and people are honest and reputable, you
don't need 500-page documents."

After the lawsuit, Mark was one of three franchisees on a committee
trying to work out a new franchise agreement and basis for trust in the
Meineke system.

"I give a huge amount of credit to Ken Walker, the president who came
into this situation and did a lot to defuse it," Mark says. "I give equal credit
to the franchisees themselves who recognized that (the lawsuit) was a business problem that was now over and it was time to get on with life. A lot
of us franchisees are small-business people so we tend, by nature, to take
things more personally."

In 2001, Meineke received a fair franchising seal from the American
Association of Franchisees and Dealers, which was approved by more than
75 percent of the Meineke franchisees. Some unhappy franchisees left the

system rather than sign the new agreement, and some who remain still distrust the franchisor, Mark says.

Still, the franchise relationship at Meineke has improved remarkably from the lawsuit days, Mark says. The company is allowing franchisees to take an active role in some decisions, such as advertising. When headquarters proposed a summer vehicle checkup special, it got franchisees on a conference telephone call to hammer out details like the price.

"By contractual rights, the company still has the ultimate right in many cases to decide how the money will be spent," Mark says. But "their approach for quite a while has been that as franchisees develop more skill, the company allows us to do more. We try to do a lot of measuring of results (of advertising). That leads the franchisor to greater willingness to try things and fail occasionally."

The franchisor sometimes modifies the franchise agreement in response to well-reasoned arguments from the franchisees, he adds. For example, headquarters agreed to reduce its royalty on some low-profit margin services, such as towing customers' vehicles or doing emissions testing, Mark says. The franchisees have agreed to the company's request to make attendance to at least one of its conventions mandatory.

"We have to keep working on it. There are still times we have heated discussions, but Meineke is living up to everything it promised. They go out of their way to meet with franchisees," he says. "In negotiations, I say that both sides come to the point that they're satisfied with the result."

92. GET INTO FRANCHISE LEADERSHIP

Franchisees should take advantage of their system's advisory council and other opportunities for involvement in company decision making.

■ ■ ■

Dan Boyle had a software development company in the 1990s and was looking around for a different opportunity. He made a wish list of the perfect business and finally bought a franchise for a Tutor Time child care center in 1995. In spite of a great deal of research, Dan was buying into a tumultuous situation. The company was selling more franchises than it had the capabilities to open. Instead of opening centers within 18 months of paying the franchise fee as promised, franchisees were waiting years. Dan's center in Laguna Niguel, California, didn't open until 2001. In 1996, 40 franchisees sued and the Federal Trade Commission fined the company $220,000 for deceptive practices and misrepresentations in its offering circular.

"I had a clause in my contract that I could back out if my center was not open in two years," Dan says. "It was supposed to be a turnkey situation with them finding the location. It never happened that way. I gave myself another year, looked for a site and developer to make it happen on my own."

He stayed with Tutor Time because he didn't know how to write curriculum and had judged originally that Tutor Time's was the best.

Tutor Time franchisees had formed a council, but Dan didn't want to be a part of it because it was adversarial. "I said I would join when the group was a more constructive body," Dan says.

The Tutor Time Franchisee Association membership changed so Dan eventually did become a member and officer of the group. "In all my approach to things, it's not just how to solve Dan's problem but the bigger issue of how to benefit all," he says. "I started roundtables for franchisees all over the United States. We would talk on the phone for an hour sharing best practices and learning from each other. The franchisees were the ones who kept it going even when the infrastructure of the company was no more than the passion of the franchisees."

A growing number of franchises have franchisee advisory councils. The most effective have independent councils whose members are selected by the franchisees themselves to truly represent their view not to rubber stamp the franchisor's dictates. Some councils draw in many members for subcommittees on such issues as advertising.

Tutor Time's troubles weren't over. It filed for bankruptcy protection in 2002. Franchisees went to the bankruptcy court hearings and spent time with attorneys and bidders for the company. New chief executive Bill Davis stabilized the company, arranged the sale to Childtime Learning Centers, and negotiated a new franchise agreement with the franchisees. Dan wasn't an official negotiator but he advised the committee. (The parent company's name changed to Learning Care Group, Inc. in 2003.)

"Bill said he wanted the new agreement to benefit both sides," Dan says. "We said if this company is going to be run by different management, we franchisees want a seat on the company board of directors, so franchisees can have a say in running the company."

That seat was granted and in 2004, Dan took the franchisee board seat. "When I had a computer consulting business, I would go into clients and ask what they wanted, how they did things. I'm used to asking questions. That's what I do with my fellow franchisees," Dan says. Even before joining the board, "I would see things that I thought Tutor Time could do better, and I would keep notes on that. Involvement in the council and the board takes a lot of time. I couldn't do that if I didn't have a great staff at my school. It's a collective effort."

93. FRANCHISE DISAGREEMENTS CHASE CUSTOMERS AWAY

If franchisees and franchisors are at odds, customers are likely
to find out and possibly take their business to a less contentious
competitor.

■ ■ ■

Bob Davis has been a distributor of emergency medical equipment since the mid-1970s. In 1994, Equipment Management Service and Repair Inc. approached Bob and other distributors about becoming franchisees. They would repair equipment for emergency services, funeral homes, long-term care facilities, dentists, and hospitals as well as warranty, repair, and preventive maintenance services on behalf of equipment manufacturers. EMSAR franchisees handle service and repairs for dozens of companies, either on an exclusive contract or as an authorized provider. In 1994, Bob agreed to be the franchisee in Holmes, New York, later expanding his territory into all of New York State, Connecticut, and part of Pennsylvania.

"My attitude on the whole concept of franchising is that the franchisor should facilitate the franchisee's running of the business. The franchisor is nothing without the franchisees," Bob says. "If the relationship between the franchisor and franchisee is not a positive one, and either side is not getting what it should, it doesn't work."

A few years ago, EMSAR had a contentious relationship with franchisees that affected business. The franchisor signed national contracts to do warranty repairs that the franchisees said they lacked the skill to do and for prices at which they could not make a profit. "Several franchisees said they were not going to do that work because it was not cost effective," Bob says.

Disagreements between franchisors and franchisees are not unusual, even among those where two-way consultation is the standard. The problem can be worse if one side acts unilaterally in a way the other side believes is detrimental to the individual or to the system. Sometimes such disagreements are low key and private. Sometimes they make news headlines because of lawsuits or other public actions. Although the EMSAR dispute didn't go that far, the medical equipment industry is small enough that customers found out about the disagreement. Some took their service and repair business elsewhere. "Word gets around fast in this industry," Bob says. "Competitors went around saying there were problems at EMSAR, and they could do the work. Rumors were all around."

While the franchisees explored their options, the franchisor brought in a new president, Renee LaPine, who had previously worked at EMSAR and had good relationships with the franchisees. "She was a positive, known entity. She always understands that we are partners," Bob says. "Her background was accounting, and she looked at potential contracts from the view of both the franchisor and franchisee, what they would cost and the return on investment. We went forward in a positive way because of that perspective."

The disputed warranty contracts were terminated by mutual consent between the manufacturer and the franchise, Bob says. Some franchisees were able to sign local contracts because they had the capabilities to do the work, but their rates were higher than the franchisor had negotiated.

The relationship between EMSAR franchisor and its franchisees is improving, Bob says. "In the past, communication was not acceptable. Now we meet on a regular basis by teleconference and discuss what is going on and what we can do to make it better."

94. FRANCHISING ISN'T FOR EVERY INDIVIDUAL

Individuals should research the franchisor and their own skills
and goals before buying a franchise. There is not a franchise
match for every potential buyer.

■ ■ ■

Derek Quinn had worked in the semiconductor industry for more
than a quarter of a century when he was forced to retire in 2003. He and
his wife decided they would like to find a business they could run together. With the assistance of a business broker, the Quinns bought a franchise in Laguna Niguel, California, for V2K Window Fashions Inc. By
2005 they and the franchisor signed a mutual release terminating the franchise contract.

Not every franchise relationship succeeds. A few cases involve fraud
or bankruptcy on one side or the other. But more commonly the problem is
a mismatch of personality or expectations. This problem puts an exclama-
tion point on experts' caution that potential franchisees ought to investigate before they invest, and franchisors should define the type of person
best suited to their systems before selling a franchise. Every franchisor/
franchisee divorce is unique, but Derek's story has some typical elements.

When the idea of buying a franchise came up, Derek focused on the
low cost of getting started. He didn't consider how different the semiconductor industry was from selling window coverings to individual consumers in their own homes. He also didn't consider that although he had
management experience, he was not an experienced sales closer. Before
buying a franchise, "ensure you feel comfortable with the initial primary
role you'll need to take to be successful," he says. "For example, if you
need to sell directly to clients, ensure you will be able to market and advertise cost effectively and that you will feel comfortable dealing with the expectations of a variety of clients consistent with the product or service you
will be selling them."

Derek says he should have done a great deal more independent research by talking to many different franchisees, including any who had left
the system. "I listened primarily to the business broker who had owned

several franchises in his business career. I also looked over Web-based ratings of franchises and did a cost analysis," he says. That cost analysis paid too little attention to the need for a new franchisee to have a financial cushion to survive three years with little income as the new business gets up and running. "It can take even longer if you don't have the background you need," he adds.

He also ignored the fact that most franchise agreements are written to favor the franchisor. Some franchisors have a take-it-or-leave-it attitude about the contract. Some will negotiate certain aspects of the agreement, but more common is the willingness only to negotiate with a franchisee advisory group so that contracts are uniform throughout the system. Regardless, "have a lawyer review the franchise agreement before you sign it," Derek says.

Perhaps most typical of Derek's experience was that he did not get the support he expected, even though he says it was probably what was promised. "You need to know exactly what the franchisor needs and why, plus what they can and will do to help you," he says. "The franchise we bought into is not supportive enough to develop a viable business for a variety of reasons including our background, cost structure, and fees. If the support staff for the franchisor is not at least one support person to every five franchisees, you learn the business from a book."

Terminating the franchise agreement early cost Derek tens of thousands of dollars including forfeited franchise fees and attorney's bills. The franchisor wanted to prevent the Quinns from running a similar business, but California does not enforce these noncompete clauses, so the Quinns now operate the independent OC Interior Fashions selling carpeting as well as window coverings.

PART 3

EXPERTS

∎ ∎ ∎

While reading about the real-world experiences of franchisors and franchisees is helpful in understanding how this relationship works, it also helps to take a step back and see franchising from the view of experts who aren't actual parties to the franchising relationship. In this section, you will see the challenges and opportunities from a different angle. You may discover conflicts and partnerships not specifically addressed in the first two parts of the book.

In this section, the top government franchise regulator, trade association executives, a franchise broker, and attorneys describe franchising issues with which they frequently deal. These experts have played important roles in the evolution of franchising in the United States. One important change has been the increased government regulation of franchise sales. Another is the move from virtual dictatorial control by franchisors with a corresponding adversarial relationship to widespread efforts to make the relationship more collaborative.

Make no mistake; franchising has its disagreements just as all forms of contractual relationships do. Some of these experts represent one side or the other. The others are in the middle trying to balance the needs for maximum benefit for the parties and the general public. When franchising works, it builds personal wealth and economic growth. Making it work is the responsibility of all the people who make their livelihood in franchising.

95.   STEVEN TOPOROFF

Franchise Rule coordinator, Federal Trade Commission

■ ■ ■

When attorney Steven Toporoff joined the Federal Trade Commission in 1988, one of his first cases involved franchising, and his interest and involvement grew until, in 1993, he was assigned as coordinator of the Federal Franchise Rule.

The U.S. government's role in franchising focuses on fraud in the initial sale of franchises, he explains. Full disclosure of all pertinent information is the goal. The fairness of the deal to both sides and the ongoing relationship are up to the buyer and seller. If things go wrong later, the FTC often leaves the resolution to contract law between the franchisor and franchisees.

The FTC receives several hundred franchising complaints each year, Steve says. It keeps a database of these complaints and, since 1997, has linked the database to local and state law enforcement agencies. Usually the FTC will conduct a free search of its database for complaints about a franchisor.

"By far, the most common issue that comes up in complaints to us is earning claims," Steve says. "There's nothing wrong with making those claims, but the franchisor must have a reasonable basis for those claims and put in its disclosure documents the methodology used in coming up with the claims."

A second common complaint relates to lack of support. "Whether it's advertising, computer systems, training, you name it, if it wasn't what the franchisee expected, he believes he was lied to," he says.

Another common complaint is "encroachment." The franchisor either doesn't give an exclusive territory to franchisees or sells units that in the franchisee's mind are too close together. The franchisor claims "the more the merrier;" consumers come to recognize the brand and everyone wins. The franchisee sees too much competition and dwindling profits for him.

The requirement to buy products or services from the franchisor is often a complaint. "Franchisors want to assure uniformity. Franchisees often complain they could buy something cheaper and just as good," Steve says. "As long as the requirement is disclosed beforehand as well as whether the franchisor gets money from the product sales, it's hard to argue that the franchisee didn't know."

Those kinds of disagreements illustrate why someone should read and fully understand the required disclosure documents and offering circulars before buying a franchise, Steve says. "Probably the most useful information in those documents is the list of franchisees, phones, and addresses. Talk to them. Visit them. A lot can be done by simple observation of their businesses. We always recommend that an individual have someone knowledgeable about franchise law look over the contract and raise questions before signing."

Outright fraud is rare in franchising "unlike business opportunities where we find significant fraud," Steve says.

(Franchises have a brand name, ongoing training and support, and a system for operating the business. Business opportunity doesn't have a trademark or brand name, support, or ongoing royalty and advertising fees. The licensee of the business opportunity is often selling the seller's products but can also sell others' products or services.)

The more common circumstance in franchising is a mom-and-pop business that draws up contracts to allow others to run businesses similar to theirs. "They sell a business arrangement with no clue that it really is a franchise arrangement. There are also franchisors who, overall, comply with the Franchise Rule but may not do some things in the correct manner."

If the FTC identifies a pattern of fraud by a franchisor causing considerable harm to franchise buyers, the commission's lawyers may file a lawsuit seeking an injunction to stop the behavior and repayment of money, Steve says. "Sometimes, if there is no fraud and no one was harmed, especially if it's a new company or it was inadvertent, we work with the company. We don't go around suing every company; the goal is to make the company come into compliance with the Franchise Rule."

96. MATTHEW SHAY

President, International Franchise Association

■ ■ ■

Attorney Matthew Shay has worked for the International Franchise Association—the oldest and largest trade association for franchisors, suppliers, and, more recently, franchisees—since 1993. In 2005, he assumed the top job for the group and has familiarity with the successes and challenges of franchising.

"Franchising is a concept that is uniquely American in the way it blends intellectual property and entrepreneurial vision of the franchisor with the passion, skills, financial resources, and sweat equity of the franchisee," Matt says. "It is an interdependent relationship in which each plays a vital role in the success of the enterprise. One cannot exist without the other."

Some mistakenly believe that franchising is a guarantee of success for anyone who tries it. But not every franchising company or every franchisee succeeds, and many individuals are not suited to be franchisees, Matt says. "If you are highly independent, highly entrepreneurial, and highly visionary, being a franchisee might not be the way to go.

"Too few people recognize that it is the franchisor's principal objective to serve as the steward of the brand and the concept. The franchisor operates at the macro, 30,000-foot level, thinking strategically about positioning the brand," he explains. "The responsibility of the franchisee is at the local level to implement and execute the brand. The most effective concepts and products come from the franchisees back to the franchisor because franchisees are closest to the customers.

"It is a circular relationship, not hierarchical," he says. "Both constantly help each other improve."

Franchising went through a period when many viewed the relationship as adversarial, that if the franchisor won, the franchisee lost and vice versa.

"I think the dialogue has moved away from franchisor versus franchisee and more toward mutual franchising interests," Matt says. "It has come about through some education and maturation on both sides. I like to think that IFA membership has played a leading role in fostering an environment that operates with honest discussion, inclusion, and openness.

"That doesn't mean that there won't always be disputes just as there are in any business relationship."

Another challenge facing business format franchising in which IFA plays a leading role is regulation by federal and state governments. Historically, Matt says, the federal government, through the Federal Trade Commission, has emphasized full disclosure of information prior to a person buying a franchise and selective enforcement of franchisors that systematically violate disclosure requirements. More than a dozen states also regulate franchising and tend to take a more aggressive approach. They require franchisors to file their offering circulars and other information prior to selling franchises in those states. "It can be extremely time consuming and expensive to do business in those states," Matt says.

The IFA wants government to make distinctions between a business-format franchise and a business opportunity. The former involves a brand name, a system of operation, and ongoing support and royalties. The latter usually sells a product or equipment but does not require their licensees to use a brand or pay ongoing royalties, and usually provides little, if any, support. The FTC has required the same disclosure from both franchisors and business-opportunity sellers, Matt says, but the states have more regulations for business opportunities. California, for example, has started expediting registrations of well-established franchisors that pose the least risk to investors and devoting more oversight to new, unknown franchisors and business opportunities, a practice that IFA wants other states to adopt, Matt says. "We think the regulatory format that places the emphasis on providing information in advance so investors understand their rights and responsibilities puts the emphasis in the right place."

97. DON DEBOLT

Former president, International Franchise Association 1995–2005

■ ■ ■

Don DeBolt, publisher of *CEO Update* in Alexandria, Virginia, was the top paid executive at the International Franchise Association for a decade. The IFA board had previously decided to be the true "voice of franchising," as it calls itself, by admitting franchisees as members, and it was Don's job to implement that change.

"I still credit IFA's decision to make franchisees an important part of the organization for bringing a cooperative, win-win, let's-work-it-out, no-surprises approach to franchising," Don says. "As more and more franchisors used that approach it spread like wildfire. A second important factor was that more franchisors became franchisees and vice versa. That hadn't been common before. More people realized they had an interest in making the relationship work."

That change came about during Don's tenure at IFA. He acknowledges that in the early 1990s a few well-known, national brands had highly publicized battles between franchisor and franchisees, and some effective franchisee advocates energized the debate that led to 30 states at least considering laws "that would constrict franchising and possibly bury it."

While some say the franchising relationship is adversarial, Don disagrees. "I think the franchise relationship is naturally harmonious. It has elements in the relationship that can lead to adversarial situations, but basically franchisors and franchisees are interdependent. Franchising's strength is the ability to aggressively purse market opportunities for franchisors who are financially limited. Franchisees have the ability to deliver the people and money to build the system. On the flip side, a system has a lot of independently owned businesses and getting them all to march in step can be like herding cats. Many systems have especially sophisticated franchisees whose companies are larger than many franchisors and they have a lot of business acumen. They may see things differently. Getting everyone going in the same direction at the same time is difficult."

Don saw tremendous change in the franchising relationship during his decade at IFA. "Both franchisors and franchisees experienced a rapid maturing process with a better understanding of what each had contributed to the success of their systems. I think franchisors have a renewed sense of the wisdom of avoiding problems with their franchisees later on by making wise choices up front. Years ago, there was a lot of 'he's got a wallet and he's breathing; sell him a franchise.' Now many franchisors realize that finding the right fit leads to a long-term, positive experience that is in everyone's best interest."

He believes one factor that improved the professionalism on both sides of the table was IFA's certification that both franchisors and franchisees have been encouraged to obtain.

Don predicts that franchising can solve some difficult problems, such as the growing need for health care and better education in the United States. "Franchising can bring solutions to that area, just as it has in other areas, for example fast food franchises helped establish standards for cleanliness and safety that reached new levels of consumer protection," Don says. "I was visiting Malaysia a few years ago, and one of the ministers told me he loved franchising. He said he saw what McDonald's and other franchisors had brought to his country in cleanliness, and competition forced those standards on the locals."

98. ROBERT PURVIN

Chairman, American Association of Franchisees and Dealers

■ ■ ■

Bob Purvin started his legal career representing franchisors—as do the overwhelming number of attorneys in the American Bar Association's franchise forum—because that is where the money is. He started recognizing that, for franchisees, franchising was neither business ownership nor safe as it was widely advertised. He founded the American Association of Franchisees & Dealers in San Diego, California, to deal with what he saw as inequities. At first, he thought new laws would level the playing field, but quickly determined that free-market solutions were better for everyone. "Any legislation would come out the other end at best a much compromised version, and the burden would likely fall on franchisees," he says.

The first issue Bob tackled was stopping the common practice of franchisors claiming that 95 percent of franchises are successful, a much greater success rate than small business as a whole. The statistic had come from unproven claims that only 1 percent of franchisees fail per year, so in five years, only 5 percent fail, Bob says. Some independent studies had found that franchisees had a higher failure rate than independent businesses. Part of the reason for this was that franchisors wouldn't count a franchise as a failure as long as they could resell it and keep the doors open. Bob says one major franchise, which claimed a 98 percent success rate, had sold 5,000 franchises, but only had 2,000 open stores. "You do the math," he says.

AAFD brought the three major influence groups—franchisors, franchisees, and lawyers—together to create standards of fair franchising that ideally would become the basis of all franchising contracts. Each standard had to be approved by a majority of representatives of each interest group on the AAFD Standards Committee and by two-thirds of the whole committee. The group had adopted 135 standards by 2005. Franchisors who meet those standards and the approval of their franchise network earn AAFD's Seal of Fair Franchising. These accredited franchisors have become AAFD's strongest supporters.

"When we started, we were rightly recognized as franchisee oriented, but today we are seen as equally loyal to franchisors and franchisees," Bob says. "Granted, most of the standards were drafted to protect franchisees.

Now we're going back and changing the wording 'obligation of the franchisor' to 'obligation of the parties.'"

Bob and AAFD push for two basic features in a franchise: a strong, independent franchisee association and a contract negotiated with the association. Obviously a franchisor can't be put in a position of negotiating every agreement individually or it cannot sustain the system, which is one of franchising's strengths, Bob says.

"I believe in franchising. What we promote is 'Total Quality Franchising,' which is a win for all sides," Bob says.

Franchising has come a long way from the inequities Bob identified in the early 1990s, but franchisees still come to him with complaints about their organizations.

"The biggest problem is lack of franchisor support," Bob says. "For most franchisees that translates into lack of market penetration." Without a sufficient number of franchisees in a geographic area, it's difficult to build brand recognition and an effective advertising program, which are two other basic strengths of franchising. "Lack of support also translates into the mediocrity factor," Bob says. "The franchisor doesn't provide the help franchisees need to succeed."

Another common problem is the use of marketing or advertising funds to which franchisees are required to contribute but have no say in spending, Bob says.

"Purchasing is the biggest area of abuse," he says. "Some franchisors treat them as profit centers. They require a franchisee to buy through approved suppliers from whom they get rebates. The franchisee could buy the products cheaper at Costco."

99. HOWARD BASSUK

Founder, FranNet

■ ■ ■

In 1987, after a career in the computer industry, Howard Bassuk looked at the franchising method of doing business and observed a gap that was a business opportunity for him. Franchising had attracted so many different companies in so many different industries that there are more franchise sellers than buyers. At the same time, those who are considering the purchase of a franchise encounter an overwhelming number of choices. What franchising needed was a matchmaker. Howie created The Franchise Network Group (FranNet) in Carlsbad, California, one of the largest networks of franchise brokers who shepherd individuals through franchise exploration and purchase. These broker-consultants are a growing part of franchising, which is even larger than when FranNet first started.

"I get asked all the time, 'What's the best franchise?' I always say, 'for whom?'" Howie says. "Part of the selection process is being brutally honest about what you're good at, what you're willing to do, your lifestyle issues."

The would-be franchisee must first define what he's looking for before he proceeds to the hard work of investigating the options that might fit that definition, Howie says. One of basic facts that FranNet stresses with these prospects is that one acceptable answer is not to buy any franchise.

"Going into business is not for everyone," Howie says. "It's not that you should or shouldn't buy a franchise. You should look in an objective way so you know what is available. You can cut risk down; you don't eliminate it. You understand what you have to do, what you can do in relative safety.

"A good decision isn't 'yes.' It's to get what you want. An ill-informed decision is not the way to do that."

Through FranNet, as with other brokers, prospective franchise buyers define what they're good at and what they enjoy doing, how much money they want to spend and how much they want to make, how long they want to own a franchise and how big they want their business to grow. These factors help narrow the field of potential purchases to two to four companies.

"We don't say 'here's a hot franchise; buy it.' We say, 'here's a proven research technique for selecting the right franchise for you,'" Howie says. "Companies go up and down. Great old companies all of a sudden are gone. So it's not enough to buy a franchise because that company was once great."

The prospect should do a great deal of research of each franchise before deciding whether and what to buy.

Perhaps the most common mistake these buyers make is buying without researching, Howie says. "To me that's the cardinal sin. There is no reason why someone should do that. It's sheer foolishness."

Another common mistake is to equate the amount of money a franchise costs with its relative value as a business opportunity, he says. On the other hand, it is equally a mistake to believe the lowest priced franchise is best because they're all the same. The right approach is to spend just the money you need to reach your goals.

Some prospects don't like the first franchises they investigate. They should look at the ways in which those franchises did not conform to what they thought they wanted, Howie says. That analysis can help adjust the model of what they are seeking.

"We have one absolute with buyers: Never settle," Howie says. "If this is not a business that gives you what you want and has other people who have already achieved what you want, why buy it?"

100. LORI M. LOFSTROM

Franchisors' attorney, Holmes & Lofstrom, LLP

■ ■ ■

Between them, Long Beach, California, law partners Lori Lofstrom and David Holmes have almost half a century of experience with franchising. David worked with franchisors and even owned a franchise before opening his law practice. Lori has chaired the California State Bar Association's Franchise Law Committee. They specialize in working the franchisor side of the fence, but it might seem they are reluctant advisors. The partners won't accept a franchising client until putting him through a half-hour tour of all the pitfalls and costs of franchising. If he still wants to franchise, he still might not be ready.

New franchisors should first put together their system model, working with consultants to write manuals, create a training program, and establish a sales process for all prospects before hiring attorneys and accountants to prepare their Uniform Franchise Offering Circular, Lori advises. "It's probably not a bad idea to meet with a lawyer and accountant to get some preliminary advice to avoid mistakes, but don't start the document drafting until you're ready. So many come in to our office and want to know how soon we can have the documents ready for them, thinking that the sooner they get their documents, the sooner they will have revenue from sales. Most are far from ready themselves to undertake this project and have not begun to put in place the systems that will be described in the legal documents."

Franchising can be a great way for a company to expand its brand and business operations with less cost and liability than in-house growth, mergers, or acquisitions, Lori says. "Franchisors can create a very valuable business if they take the time and make the investment to set a system up properly and maintain compliance."

However, franchising is not trouble-free, she adds. "Franchise litigation is quite common and can easily cripple a franchise system. Earnings claims, encroachment, trademark infringement, and misrepresentation are some of the favorite causes of action." Laws are not uniform from state to state or internationally, and a franchisor, even with the best intentions, can be severely punished, she says.

In fact, the ever-increasing laws and regulations on franchising are the biggest challenge, Lori says. "Legal compliance with the federal and state franchise and business opportunity regulations, advertising laws, registration and disclosure processes, earnings claims, (and so on) make complying with the franchise laws like running a gauntlet of 'gotchas.' These regulations require specialized counsel making continued compliance quite expensive."

Most new franchisors are surprised by the legal and accounting costs of preparing documents and financial statements and the detail required for the Uniform Franchise Offering Circular, Lori says. These newbies expect to be partners with their franchisees, and psychologically, that's a good approach, she says. "On a legal level, however, nothing could be further from reality, and such a structure would be one of the least desirable for a franchise system" because of the franchising laws.

"My favorite piece of advice to franchisors sounds trite but it cannot be overstated. Have adequate capitalization," Lori says. "A franchisor that is not adequately capitalized will be too hungry for its first sales and will tend to sign up initial franchisees if they are breathing and have funds. These first franchisees are so critical to a system as these will be the folks that all of a franchisor's future prospects will get their validation from, and they need to be well-qualified, financially stable entrepreneurs who can follow a system. If a franchisor is desperate for cash, it will overlook some serious deficiencies (in the buyer), and that will come back to haunt the franchise for many years to come."

101. W. MICHAEL GARNER

Franchisees' attorney, Dady & Garner, P.A.

■ ■ ■

After becoming an attorney in 1975, Michael Garner represented both sides of franchising. Then in 1994, Michael Dady started a new law firm in Minneapolis, Minnesota, to represent franchisees exclusively and asked Michael Garner to join him. They formed Dady & Garner, P.A. in 1997.

Franchisees can make a great deal of money with a good product or service and a strong brand, but the financial interests of franchisees and franchisors are not perfectly balanced, Michael says. "The franchisor makes its profits on the basis of the franchisee's gross revenues. The franchisee does not have to be profitable for the franchisor to get its money. The franchisor's interest is in getting the franchisee to invest heavily and build a revenue machine; the franchisee's interest is in being profitable. Simple example: A (fast-food) franchisor wants to drive sales by offering dollar meals; a franchisee can't make a profit on a dollar meal," he says. "How do you balance these competing interests? The franchisor depends on the franchisee for investment of capital, risk taking, and hiring of employees. If the franchisee is successful, they both benefit. If the franchisee fails, the franchisor has no out-of-pocket loss or at least none that approaches the franchisee's loss."

Most franchisors don't dislike their franchisees or unduly exploit them, Michael says, but franchisors naturally put their own interest first. The franchise buyer must be on guard for that fact. "The franchisees' first line of defense is information. They should be soberly self-informed," he says. "I see it all the time. People go to buy a house, and they go to a lot of open houses, ask a lot of questions, and get a home inspection. They go to buy a car, and they read *Consumer Reports* and test drive a lot of models. But in franchising, somebody comes to them with a concept, they fall in love and don't even shop around. They'll take more care with the purchase of a $20,000 car than a $200,000 franchise.

"Don't fall in love," he emphasizes. "This is a business, not a romance."

Michael believes the biggest franchisor abuse is fraud or misrepresentation during the sale. "There's more overreaching and overselling of franchises than you would find in other walks of life. I would rather buy a used car. A lot of franchises are sold on a commission so you have a lot of salespeople whose self-interest is in selling the franchise and will do what they have to do to make the sale."

A second major problem facing franchisees in concepts that have been around a while is oversaturation, Michael says. To satisfy owners or shareholders, franchisors need to keep building revenues. The obvious way to do that is to sell more franchises. "For some there's no more room to build more units so what you see some mature concepts doing is either putting units closer together—encroaching on existing franchisees' territory—or trying to extend the brand into other concepts."

As an example of the first problem Michael cites Pizza Hut's move in the 1990s to add take-out and home-delivery locations to its chain of sit-down restaurants. An example of the second problem was Carvel, which has ice cream parlors, selling ice cream cakes through supermarkets in the 1990s. Some franchisees sued for breach of contract and federal courts agreed.

Michael believes franchising can be a wonderful means of distribution, but cautions would-be franchisees to look for a franchise that has something truly proprietary, such as patented products, and a strong brand name. "It's easy to franchise a concept, have an agreement, file for a trademark," he says. "The hard part is having a business that in the long term is going to sell. Everyone claims they're going to be the McDonald's of their industry segment. The fact is nobody is."

THE UNIFORM FRANCHISE OFFERING CIRCULAR

The Federal Trade Commission requires franchisors to disclose certain information to potential buyers at least ten days prior to signing a franchise contract or paying any money. The information that must be disclosed in the Uniform Franchise Offering Circular includes:

1. Franchisor's formal corporate name and state of incorporation, background, and any predecessor companies and affiliates
2. Past five years of business experience of the franchisor's key executives
3. Details of pertinent litigation in the previous ten years involving the franchisor or its officers
4. Any bankruptcy in the previous ten years of the franchisor, a predecessor company, or executives
5. Initial franchise fee
6. Other fees, royalties, expenses
7. Total investment to open the franchise
8. Requirements to buy or lease products or services through the franchisor or designated suppliers
9. Any financing the franchisor provides
10. Obligations of the franchisor
11. Description of territorial rights, if any
12. Any trademarks or logos and whether they are legally protected
13. Whether the franchisor owns patents, copyrights, or other proprietary information
14. Whether the franchisee can be an absentee owner or is required to be at the business location
15. Any restrictions on products or services the franchisee can sell

16. How franchise contract renewals, terminations, sale or transfer, and dispute resolutions are handled
17. Whether any celebrities or public figures are involved in promoting the franchise
18. Earnings claims (not mandatory)
19. Names and contact information of current franchisees and those who have left the system within the previous year, as well as three-year growth of the number of franchisees and anticipated growth in the coming year
20. Franchisor's audited financial statements and balance sheet for previous three years
21. Copies of contracts the franchisee must sign
22. Acknowledgement that the franchisee received a copy of the disclosure documents

INTERNATIONAL FRANCHISE ASSOCIATION CODE OF ETHICS (SUMMARY)

Preface: The International Franchise Association Code of Ethics is intended to establish a framework for the implementation of best practices in the franchise relationships of IFA members . . . The IFA's members believe that adherence to the values expressed in the IFA Code will result in healthy, productive and mutually beneficial franchise relationships.

Every franchise relationship is founded on the mutual commitment of both parties to fulfill their obligations under the franchise agreement. Each party will fulfill its obligations, will act consistent with the interests of the brand and will not act so as to harm the brand and system . . .

. . . IFA's members are committed to showing respect and consideration for each other and to those with whom they do business . . . IFA members believe that franchisors and franchisees share the responsibility for improving their franchise system in a manner that rewards both franchisors and franchisees.

. . . To foster franchising as a unique and enormously successful relationship, IFA's members commit to establishing and maintaining programs that promote effective communication within franchise systems.

IFA's members enthusiastically support full compliance with, and vigorous enforcement of, all applicable federal and state franchise regulations . . .

IFA's members are realistic about franchise relationships, and recognize that from time to time disputes will arise in those relationships. IFA's members are committed to the amicable and prompt resolution of these disputes . . . The IFA also strongly recommends the use of the National Franchise Mediation Program (NFMP) when a more structured mediation service is needed to help resolve differences.

FRANCHISEE BILL OF RIGHTS

American Association of Franchisees and Dealers

The franchisees of America do proclaim this Franchisee Bill of Rights as the minimum requirements of a fair and equitable franchise system:

- The right to an equity in the franchised business, including the right to meaningful market protection
- The right to engage in a trade or business, including a post-termination right to compete
- The right to the franchisor's loyalty, good faith, and fair dealing, and due care in the performance of the franchisor's duties, and a fiduciary relationship where one has been promised or created by conduct
- The right to trademark protection
- The right to full disclosure from the franchisor, including the right to earnings data available to the franchisor which is relevant to the franchisee's decision to enter or remain in the franchise relationship
- The right to initial and ongoing training and support
- The right to competitive sourcing of inventory, product, service, and supplies
- The right to reasonable restraints upon the franchisor's ability to require changes within the franchise system
- The right to marketing assistance
- The right to associate with other franchisees
- The right to representation and access to the franchisor
- The right to local dispute resolution and protection under the laws and the courts of the franchisee's jurisdiction

- A reasonable right to renew the franchise
- The reciprocal right to terminate the franchise agreement for reasonable and just cause, and the right not to face termination, unless for cause

RESOURCES

The following companies, agencies, professional organizations, and Web sites provide information about and assistance with franchising.

American Association of Franchisees & Dealers—Trade association that advocates "total quality franchising" with fairness to franchisees; members include franchisors, franchisees, and attorneys; P.O. Box 81887, San Diego, CA 92138-1887, 800-733-9858, http://www.aafd.org

American Bar Association Forum on Franchising—Subgroup of the American Bar Association for attorneys who specialize in franchise law, http://www.abanet.org/forums/franchising

American Franchisee Association—Trade association advocates for franchisees and dealers; developed the Model Responsible Franchise Practices Act; 53 West Jackson Boulevard, Suite 1157, Chicago, IL 60604, 312-431-0545, http://www.franchisee.org

Entrepreneur Magazine—Publishes an annual list of the top 500 franchising companies, available in the magazine, in book form, and online at http://www.entrepreneur.com

The Entrepreneur's Source—Franchise broker that helps prospects evaluate and select a franchise to buy, service is free to the prospect, 3333 Walnut Street, Boulder, CO 80301-2515, 720-548-5000, http://www.esource.com

Federal Trade Commission—600 Pennsylvania Avenue, NW, Washington, DC 20580, 202-326-2222, http://www.ftc.gov

Franchise Opportunities Guide—Semiannual publication of information about franchising and basic information and contacts for companies that are currently selling franchises, published by the International Franchise Association

Franchise Registry—Online listing of franchise companies whose franchisees get streamlined review process when they apply for loans guaranteed by the U.S. Small Business Administration, http://www.franchiseregistry.com

Franchise Times—Bimonthly magazine with news and information about franchising, http://www.franchisetimes.com

Franchising World—Monthly magazine published by International Franchise Association

FranChoice—Franchise broker that helps prospects evaluate and select a franchise to buy, service is free to the prospect, http://www.franchoice.com

FranNet—Franchise broker that helps prospects evaluate and select a franchise to buy, service is free to the prospect, http://www.frannet.com

International Franchise Association—Largest trade organization for franchising with franchisors, franchisees, and suppliers among membership, 1501 K Street, NW, Suite 350, Washington, DC 20005, 202-628-8000, http://www.franchise.org

U.S. Franchise News—Online source for franchise information and updates, http://www.usfranchisenews.com

U.S. Small Business Administration—Guarantees small-business loans made by private lenders, many franchisees use these loans, 409 Third Street, SW, Washington, DC 20416, 800-U-ASK-SBA (827-5722), http://www.sba.gov

WEB SITES OF COMPANIES IN THIS BOOK

1. Hillcrest Associates, http://www.hillcrestassociates.com
2. Camp Bow Wow, http://www.campbowwowusa.com
3. Abrakadoodle, http://www.abrakadoodle.com
4. GarageTek Inc., http://www.garagetek.com
5. My Girl Friday, Inc., http://www.egirlfriday.com
6. Profit-Tell International, http://www.profit-tell.com
7. Mini-Tankers Canada, http://www.minitankers.ca
8. R.J. Gator's, http://www.rjgators.com
9. Systems Paving Inc., http://www.systemspaving.com
10. American Leak Detection, http://www.americanleakdetection.com
11. Snappy Auctions, http://www.snappyauctions.com
12. Wireless Toyz, http://www.wirelesstoyz.com
13. Expectec Technology Services, http://www.expetec.com
14. FASTSIGNS, http://www.fastsigns.com
15. Farmer Boys Food, Inc., http://www.farmerboys.com
16. Wood Re New, http://www.woodrenew.com
17. Royal Family Kids' Camps, http://www.rfkc.org
18. Old Oak Partners, LLC, http://www.oldoakpartners.com
19. Moe's Southwest Grill, http://www.moes.com; Raving Brands, http://www.ravingbrands.com
20. It's a Grind Coffee House, http://www.itsagrind.com
21. AlphaGraphics, http://www.alphagraphics.com
22. Mr. Handyman, LLC, http://www.mrhandyman.com
23. Aire Serv Heating & Air Conditioning, Inc., http://www.airserv.com; Dwyer Group, http://www.dwyergroup.com
24. U.S. Franchise Systems, Inc., http://www.usfsi.com
25. Figaro's Italian Pizza, Inc., http://www.figaros.com
26. PostNet International, http://www.postnet.com

27. LaMar's Donuts, http://www.lamars.com
28. Learning Express Inc., http://www.learningexpress.com
29. RPM Pizza, LLC, http://www.rpmpizza.com; Domino's Pizza, LLC, http://www.dominos.com
30. Rocksolid Granit USA Inc., http://www.granitetransformations.com
31. The Blind Brokers Network, http://www.myblindbiz.com
32. FranchiseBuyer, http://www.franchisebuyer.com
33. Maui Wowi, http://www.mauiwowi.com
34. Dry-B-Lo, http://www.dry-b-lo.com
35. Discovery Map International, LLC, http://www.discoverymap.com
36. U.S. Lawns, http://www.uslawns.com
37. MotoPhoto, http://www.motophoto.com
38. Marco's Pizza, http://www.marcos.com
39. The Maids International, Inc., http://www.maids.com
40. Vintage Stock, http://www.vintagestock.com; The Franchise Architects, http://www.franchisearchitects.com
41. Dickey's Barbecue Restaurants, Inc., http://www.dickeys.com
42. 1-800-GOT-JUNK?, http://www.1800gotjunk.com
43. American Ramp Systems, http://www.americanramp.com
44. SUBWAY, http://www.subway.com
45. Bark Busters, http://www.barkbusters.com
46. Ultimate Franchise Systems Inc., http://www.ufsi.com
47. Rapid Refill Ink International Corporation, http://www.rapidrefillink.com
48. Snappy Auctions, http://www.snappyauctions.com
49. FASTSIGNS, http://www.fastsigns.com
50. Cash Plus Family Financial Service Centers, http://www.cashplusinc.com
51. Handyman Network Inc., http://www.handyman-network.com
52. AlphaGraphics, http://www.alphagraphics.com
53. Action International Business Coaching, http://www.action-international.com; Action Business Coaching & Essentials, LLC, http://www.abicoaching.com
54. Express Personnel Services, http://www.expresspersonnel.com
55. Kumon Math & Reading Centers, http://www.kumon.com
56. 1-800-GOT-JUNK?, http://1800gotjunk.com
57. SUNBELT Business Brokers, http://www.sunbeltnetwork.com

58. Arbys, http://www.arbys.com; Franchise Developments, Inc., http://www. franchise-dev.com

59. Proshred Security, http://www.proshred.com

60. KidzArt, http://http://www.kidzart.com

61. SUBWAY, http://www.subway.com; Maggie Moo's Ice Cream and Treatery, http://www.maggiemoos.com; Comerica Bank, http://www.comerica.com

62. Bark Busters, http://www.barkbusters.com; FranChoice, http://nneyer.franchoice.com

63. Aaron's Sales and Lease Ownership, http://www.aaronsfranchise.com

64. Mr. Handyman, LLC, http://www.mrhandyman.com

65. The Entrepreneur's Source, http://www.theesource.com

66. Golden Corral Buffet & Grill, http://www.goldencorral.com

67. Zpizza, http://www.zpizza.com

68. FASTSIGNS, http://www.fastsigns.com

69. Mr. Transmission, http://www.mrtransmission.com

70. Gotcha Covered, http://www.gotchcoveredblinds.com

71. Kumon Math & Reading Centers, http://www.kumon.com

72. The Entrepreneur's Source, http://www.theesource.com

73. Christmas Décor, http://www.christmasdecor.net; Nite Time Décor, Inc., http://www.nitetimedecor.com

74. FranchiseKnowHow, LLC, http://www.franchiseknowhow.com

75. Sandler Sales Institute, http://www.sandler.com; Bailey Marketing, http://baileymarketing.sandler.com

76. The UPS Store, http://www.theupsstore.com

77. PostNet International, http://www.postnet.com

78. Jet-Black International, http://www.jet-black.com

79. Maggie Moo's Ice Cream and Treatery, http://www.maggiemoos.com

80. ServiceMaster Clean, http://www.ownafranchise.com

81. Home Instead Senior Care, http://www.homeinstead.com

82. ColorGlo International, http://www.colorglo.com

83. The Alternative Board, http://www.tabboards.com

84. Falcon Holdings, http://www.falconholdings.com; Church's Chicken, http://www.churchs.com

85. Valpak, http://www.valpak.com

86. PIP Printing and Document Services, http://www.pip.com

87. Action International Business Coaching, http://www.action-international.com; http://www.coachmybiz.com
88. Wireless Toyz, http://www.wirelesstoyz.com
89. Apple Spice Junction, http://www.applespice.com
90. FASTFRAME, http://www.fastframe.com
91. Meineke Car Care Centers, http://www.ownameineke.com
92. Tutor Time, http://www.tutortime.com; Learning Care Group, Inc., http://www.learningcaregroup.com
93. EMSAR, http://www.emsar.com
94. OC Fashion Interiors, http://www.ocfashions.com
95. Federal Trade Commission, http://www.ftc.gov
96. International Franchise Association, http://www.franchise.org
97. CEO Update, http://www.ceoupdate.com
98. American Association of Franchisees & Dealers, http://www.aafd.org
99. FranNet, http://www.frannet.com
100. Holmes & Lofstrom, LLP, http://www.holmeslofstrom.com
101. Dady & Garner, P.A., http://www.dadygarner.com

INDEX